SPREAD TRADING

Low-Risk Strategies for Profiting from Market Relationships

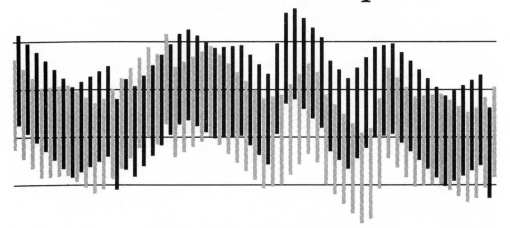

Howard Abell

Dearborn
Financial Publishing, Inc.®

This publication is designed to provide accurate and authoritative information in regard to the subject matter covered. It is sold with the understanding that the publisher is not engaged in rendering legal, accounting, or other professional service. If legal advice or other expert assistance is required, the services of a competent professional person should be sought.

Executive Editor: Cynthia A. Zigmund
Managing Editor: Jack Kiburz
Interior Design: Lucy Jenkins
Cover Design: Rafi Kushmir and Associates
Typesetting: Elizabeth Pitts

Published by Dearborn Financial Publishing, Inc.®

Printed in the United States of America

97 98 99 10 9 8 7 6 5 4 3 2 1

Library of Congress Cataloging-in-Publication Data

Abell, Howard.
　　Spread trading : low-risk strategies for profiting from market relationships / Howard Abell.
　　　　p.　cm.
　　Includes index.
　　ISBN 0-7931-2425-5
　　　　1. Futures—United States.　2. Speculation—United States.
　　3. Stockbrokers—United States—Psychology.　4. Investment analysis.
　　I. Title.
　　HG6024.U6A63　1997
　　332.64'5—dc21　　　　　　　　　　　　　　　　　　　97-8296
　　　　　　　　　　　　　　　　　　　　　　　　　　　　　　　CIP

Dedication

This book is dedicated to all traders who
have the courage to successfully pursue their goals.

When I came to the Chicago Board of Trade some 25 years ago, I soon realized that there was a unique class of trader—the spread trader. This particular type of trader, when trading March corn, for example, would also keep a close watch on the price movements in May and July corn—or perhaps the price differentials between March corn and May wheat or new crop July wheat.

Spread trading demanded great perspicacity on the part of the trader. A good spreader must be aware of not only the absolute price, but also the price relationships among different contracts, contract months, or commodities. Simply put, spread trading demanded that a trader possess the ability to keep a lot of balls in the air at the same time.

When I looked around, the successful role models I saw before me were spread traders. Accordingly, I patterned my own trading after these successful role models. I quickly learned that spreading is not for the casual trader. Spreading takes a lot of work, a great deal of concentration, and a certain degree of confidence.

It became readily apparent that the concept of spread trading did more than simply offer interesting trading opportunities. A good spreader plays an important role in the trading community, providing important market liquidity and restoring price stability following price dislocations explored in an interdelivery, intermarket, or intercommodity spread.

I was fortunate. I was able to learn how to "spread" during simpler, less turbulent times. It is far more difficult today to learn the mechanics of spread trading, to say nothing of the critical nuances of this euclidean, elegant type of trade. However, as financial and agricultural markets become more complex—and increasingly more interwoven—it is more important than ever to understand the intricacies of spread trading.

That is why this book serves a critical function in clearly delineating the mechanics of spread trading, as well as in distilling the nuances of the concept with relevant, successful trading strategies involving spreading techniques.

Spread Trading strikes me as unique in the annals of technically oriented books. Certain books are written for neophytes; others are geared toward seasoned commodity trading professionals. Despite the many books about the markets collecting dust in bookstores, there is clearly a dearth of books that encompass the range covered by *Spread Trading.* Clearly, *Spread Trading* is a volume that, once purchased, will remain on a trader's desk for a long time.

Following in a distinguished line of successful books penned by Howard Abell—including *The Innergame of Trading, The Outer Game of Trading,* and *The Day Trader's Advantage—Spread Trading* is the rare volume that services both ends of the markets. Obviously, Howard himself has learned the importance of simultaneously servicing different ends of the marketplace.

> —Patrick H. Arbor
> Chairman, Chicago Board of Trade
> March 24, 1997

"Look and you will find it—
What is unsought will go undetected."

–Sophocles

CONTENTS

Preface   viii
Acknowledgments   x

PART I
Psychological and Strategic Considerations of Spread Trading

1. The Psychology of Successful Spread Trading   3
2. Overcoming the Psychological Barriers That
   Hold Most Spread Traders Back   15
3. Strategy and the Overall Game Plan   21

PART II
Technical Analysis and Spread Trading

4. Market Analysis and Spread Trading   29
5. Seasonal, Cyclical, and Historical Spread Relationships   63

PART III
The Top Traders and Market Experts

6. F. McCoy Coan   105
7. John Newhouse   115
8. Girard Miller   127
9. Steve Moore   141
10. Margery Teller   153
11. Jeffrey L. Silverman   163

PART IV
Winning versus Losing

12. How Winning Spread Traders Think   177
13. Principles of Successful Spread Trading   187

Index   193
About the Author   197

PREFACE

I believe *Spread Trading* fills a conspicuous void in the trading literature; it tells how to formulate consistently profitable spread-trading strategies within specific asset classes (e.g., interest rates, metals, grains, stock indices, etc.), taking into consideration historical, cyclical, and seasonal factors. To the best of my knowledge, nowhere in the literature has anyone informed us about how to create an effective spread-trading system or identified what specific forms of technical and fundamental analyses are best suited for real-time spread-trading success.

Spread traders can be scalpers, day traders, or position traders; however, the techniques they utilize are substantially different from those of outright traders. The spreader focuses on the differential, that is, the difference in price between one futures contract month and another contract month, or the difference in prices between related markets (e.g., corn and wheat, gold and silver, Eurodollars and bonds). Although successful spreading strategies always involve good risk management, the unlimited possibilities of spread relationships create widely varying risk/reward ratios.

My goal in *Spread Trading* is to establish through narrative and interviews the following:

- The specific opportunities available to spread traders
- Ways spread trading can be employed to control risk and effectively resolve specific psychological issues
- Ways to utilize specific spread-trading techniques and strategies
- Ways to identify cyclical patterns and historical spread relationships for trading profits

Spread Trading addresses all of these considerations in detail. It is based on 25 years of spread-trading success, on an intimate knowledge of the psychology underlying successful trading, and on my personal work training successful traders on and off the exchange floors as a principal of a clearing firm specializing in our own proprietary traders.

I believe *Spread Trading* builds logically on the insights of my three previous books—*The Innergame of Trading* (Irwin, 1993), *The Outer Game of Trading* (Irwin, 1994), and *The Day Trader's Advantage* (Dearborn, 1996) and will provide an invaluable resource for traders to significantly strengthen their market performance.

ACKNOWLEDGMENTS

Many people contributed to the writing of *Spread Trading*. They are: F. McCoy Coan, Girard Miller, John Newhouse, Jeffrey Silverman, David Stein, Steve Moore, and Margery Teller. In particular, I wish to thank my friend and business partner, Bob Koppel, for his expert advice and guidance.

I also want to thank Cynthia Zigmund and the entire staff at Dearborn Financial Publishing. This is the second book I have written for Dearborn; their ongoing commitment to excellence and their enthusiasm for this project are once again warmly acknowledged.

P·A·R·T

I

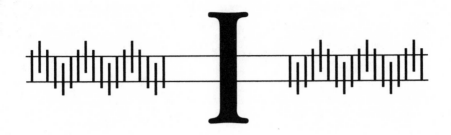

Psychological and Strategic Considerations of Spread Trading

CHAPTER 1

The Psychology of Successful Spread Trading

For most of us, the task of beating the market is not difficult, it is the job of beating ourselves that proves to be overwhelming. In this sense, beating ourselves means mastering our emotions and attempting to think independently, as well as not being swayed by those around us.

—*Martin Pring,* Investment Psychology Explained

Spread trading in one sense is exactly like outright trading and in another sense is distinctly different: the psychological component of spread trading requires all the internal rigor, commitment, and discipline of an outright long or short position. In terms of trading tactics and strategy, spread trading requires a very different set of skills.

The time horizon of a spread trader can be short- or long-term. However, the spreader focuses on one essential condition at all times: the differential, the difference in price between one futures contract month and another contract month or the difference in prices between related markets (e.g., corn and wheat, gold and silver, bonds and notes). Leo Melamed had this to say about the successful spread trader: "The professional spreader is an artist. His aptitude, agility, and ability to detect the slightest market shift is extraordinary. He is constantly active, moving as a buyer of one month to a seller of another and immediately back again. In fact, many spreaders perform this activity among three or four contract months at

The object is to pick up even the smallest increment of profit in the shift of the differential(s). The spreader is always alert to a new offer or bid on one given month that could be spread profitably into another month. He is quick to react to any sudden downdraft or updraft in the market so that he can unwind on the side of his spread for that small moment of market movement and lock it up again as soon as the price movement has stopped." (*Leo Melamed on the Markets,* Wiley, 1992.)

Most Common Types of Spread Positions

Strategy	*Example Trade*
Intracommodity spread	Long March, 98 Eurodollars
	Short June, 99 Eurodollars
Intercommodity spread	Long gold, short silver
Intermarket spread	Long S&P 500, short FTSE

Let us begin our discussion of spread trading with the most obvious of questions: Why spread trade in the first place? It seems to me, and I base this opinion on having traded spreads for more than 25 years both as a market maker on the floors of the Chicago Mercantile Exchange and the Chicago Board of Trade, that spread trading offers the following market opportunities:

- Many spreads within specific asset classes follow seasonal patterns.
- Spreads can often be defined in money management terms very specifically in terms of risk and objective in a way outright positions cannot (e.g., carrying charge spreads).
- Spreads offer a means to trade directionally in volatile markets.
- Spreads provide market opportunities in seemingly dull markets.

- Spreads can be utilized for both long- and short-term strategies as well as long and short positions.
- Spreads are routinely utilized by professionals, hedgers, and commercial traders.
- Spreads provide greater risk management and opportunity within an overall portfolio (e.g., butterflies, ratios, tandems, etc.) with specific benefits in terms of margin requirements.

The trader must keep in mind at all times that spread position strategies are always based on the concept of differential. Each strategy is based therefore on the trader's bias to market direction, seasonality, volatility, and individual performance within or outside of particular market groups. In essence, the three reasons for adapting a spread strategy can be simply stated:

1. To capture the price differential between intracommodity, intercommodity, or intermarket spreads
2. To capture the price differential based on market bias
3. To capture the price differential based on time and volatility

The trader, again, should note that the operative word here is *differential.* In fact, spreading can be costly when not considered in terms of the price differential's internal logic. Anyone who has ever been the "wrong way" on an old crop–new crop spread or an intercommodity spread understands this point all too well!

Reasons for Not Adopting a Spread Strategy

1. It's easier than taking an outright position.
2. Taking a net long and net short position always defines your risk more clearly.
3. In spreading you can't lose a lot and it's easier to get out.

4. You want to spread off a loss (prevent an open loss from becoming a realized one).
5. You decide to reduce margin requirements.
6. There's nothing outright to do.

Now that I have clearly explained the reasons for adopting a spread position as well as the reasons for not adopting a spread position, let me return to my original statement, which was that in the final analysis the psychological aspects of spreading are no different from any other form of trading, be it equities, options, cash, or futures. The challenge for the trader is to customize a trading method, approach, or system that is profitable, consistent, and personal, while navigating a trading environment whose salient character is paradox and contradiction. This is to say the trader must act with certainty in a dynamic environment where contradiction and conflicting information are the rules.

Therefore, my goals in *Spread Trading* are to (1) identify the psychological barriers that hold most traders back, (2) state the specific psychological skills that traders need to have in place in order to exploit spread-trading opportunities, (3) demonstrate the overall strategic approach required for trading success, (4) detail specific spread-trading tactics within particular asset classes that offer the highest probability of a consistently profitable return, and (5) explain the seasonal and cyclical nature of spreads and draw distinctions between intra-commodity, intercommodity, and intermarket spread trading.

Successful Trading

What follows is a presentation of what I believe to be the keys to successful trading in diagrammatic form.

The Syntax of Successful Trading

- Well-analyzed trade
- System of empowering personal beliefs and attitudes
- Proper execution based on positive focus
- Decisive, resourceful state of mind
- Successful trading performance

The Winning State of Mind

Resourceful state of mind → Strategy → Positive trading response

- Anxiety-free
- Self-trusting
- Confident
- High self-esteem

Psychological Characteristics of the Winning State of Mind

- Expect the best of yourself.
- Establish a personal standard of excellence.
- Create an internal atmosphere for success based on compelling motivation and focus.
- Communicate effectively with yourself; see yourself as positive, resourceful, and self-empowering.

Self-Defeating Attitudes Traders Possess That Guarantee Loss

- Holding yourself to impossible standards
- Trying to please others
- Thinking in absolute terms
  - black or white
  - all or nothing
  - total success or total failure
- Focusing on negative things

- Believing your childhood or past experiences have pro-
  grammed you for failure
- Demanding certainty of yourself and the market
- Defining trading as impossible
- Representing a bad trade as a catastrophe
- Labeling yourself in a globally negative way rather than
  just looking at "the trade"

Traders always speak of "getting the edge," and this is particularly true of the most successful traders. However, without
exception, the top traders understand that the edge has little to
do with the commonsense or conventional notion of getting a
good fill in the market or being stopped out exactly at your
price. Edge rather comes down to this:

- A uniquely independent strategy or approach
- A personal discipline based on hard work, independence,
  and patience
- Heightened focus and concentration
- Well-defined risk and money management
- Acceptance of losing as part of the trading process

Critical Factors in Determining a Trader's Edge

Trader Response	Having the Edge	Losing the Edge
Patience	Waits for opportunities to materialize based on well-thought-out plan	Little planning, reacts to personal whim
Discipline	Sees the big picture, responds deliberately	Emotional, anxious, often confused about what to do

Trader Response	***Having the Edge***	***Losing the Edge***
Strategy	Highly planned; limits losses, lets profits run	Little planning, does not rely on consistent methodology
Expertise	Well-prepared—has done the necessary homework	Little market knowledge; unprepared
Motive	Long-term motive, e.g., intellectual challenge	To make money, instant gratification
Goals	Clearly defined	Ill-defined
Risk Control	Highly controlled risk/reward ratio	Little or no control over risk/reward ratio
State of Mind	Positive, resourceful; empowering beliefs and focus; high level of self-esteem and trust; relaxed and confident	Nervous, anxious, believes the worst will happen; focus is distracted; trades in conflict

Well analyzed and well-strategized trade (based on probabilities)	→	Automatic execution (based on possessing the trader's edge)	→	Successful trading results (whether the trade makes or loses money)

Many good books have been written about what constitutes sound trading practices. I believe Vic Sperandeo's book, *Trader Vic: Methods of a Wall Street Master* (Wiley, 1991) is one of the best and offers the following basic rules, which should underlie any sound trading approach:

- Trade with a plan and stick to it.
- Trade with the trend.
- Use stop loss orders wherever practical.
- When in doubt, get out!
- Be patient.
- Don't overtrade.
- Let your profits run, cut losses short.
- Never let a profit run into a loss.
- Buy weakness and sell strength.
- Be just as willing to sell as to buy.
- Invest in the early stages of a bull market.
- Be a speculator in the later stages of a bull or bear market.
- Don't add to a losing position.
- Never buy or sell price.
- Trade only liquid markets.
- Reject tips.
- Analyze your mistakes.
- Never trade if your success depends on a good execution.
- Always keep your own trade records.
- **Know and follow the rules.**

It is imperative to keep these rules in mind or, more precisely, to know them intuitively, because the ultimate success or failure of your spread trading will largely be determined not by knowing a tactical nuance but rather from integrating these rules into your trading psyche.

Psychological Skills Required for Successful Spread Trading

Following are the personal tools you will need to be a successful spread trader:

- Compelling personal motivation
- Goal setting
- Confidence
- Anxiety control
- Focus
- State of mind

Let's review each skill and then relate it specifically to the demands of spread trading.

Compelling Personal Motivation

This means possessing the intensity to do whatever it takes to win at trading; to overcome a bad day or setback in order to achieve your trading goals. Think of the intensity of a world-class athlete: fully engaged and not afraid to play the game; not afraid of "being there," totally involved in the moment.

Goal Setting

Goal setting is imperative to the spread trader, not only in terms of setting realistic and measurable goals within the context of a specific time frame, but also in terms of enhancing motivation and performance. Setting goals, in fact, conditions the trader on an ongoing basis to boost his or her trading to the next level. It is excellence, not perfection, that is the point here—excellence produces results; perfection produces ulcers.

Confidence

Confidence based on competence is purely a result of motivation, belief (in oneself and the market), and state of mind. Confidence in psychological terms is not more than consistently expecting a positive outcome. Think of anything you have ever done in your life with that feeling of confidence (positive expectation). Didn't that feeling ultimately predict a successful result? The same is true with trading.

Focus

The tighter your focus, and the finer the distinctions you bring to your trading focus, the better the results. *Focus* is one of those terms that sounds like a cliché unless you understand how to utilize it in your trading. It is through focus that one stays consistent and is able to maintain a high level of confidence. Focus derives from developing a specific strategy that allows you to feel certain and act accordingly.

State of Mind

How you feel at any given moment in time will determine your state of mind, including what you feel physically, represent visually, and process emotionally about your trading. Learning how to manage your state of mind will determine whether you hesitate or act, and whether you are emotionally drained or physically and psychologically energized.

Positive Imagery

We have the power and ability to choose what imagery we process in our minds and bodies. We can literally choose the character and intensity of the images (feeling on a physical level) that are of a visual, auditory, and kinesthetic (physical) nature. We can see failure or success, trading loss or market information, paralyzing circumstances or trading opportunities. It is your mind—you run it! Following are some kinds of imagery that enhance one's trading performance.

Successful Trading Performance

Bodily Response	Visualization	Auditory
Your body feels light. Shoulders are erect, torso is straight. Facial muscles are taut, breathing is deep and relaxed. Eyes are looking straight ahead. Trader is feeling strong, energized and enthusiastic.	You are seeing yourself succeed; watching yourself in control, yet relaxed; looking competent, confident, and positive.	Yours is the voice of confidence and control, the sound of relaxed, effortless trading.

Visual Imagery That Enhances Performance

- Picturing success
- Seeing yourself in control
- Looking competent, relaxed, confident, positive
- Viewing a positive visual image that improves your performance

Auditory Imagery That Enhances Performance

- Hearing the voice of confidence
- Saying to yourself, "I knew I was right."
- Listening to the voice of positive expectation

Kinesthetic Imagery That Enhances Trading Performance

- Body feels light, confident
- Body is energized, strong
- Focus is direct and alert
- Breathing is relaxed and effortless; breaths are long and deep

Each of these psychological skills is critical for success in spread trading. Spread traders in particular must have their "eyes on the ball" of the differential—the spread trader's unique focus—at all times. It is easy to lose motivation or confidence or become distracted by price action or volatility and forget that the essential key to successful spread trading is always the same—the price difference in intramarket, intermarket, and related market relationships. To the extent that traders can integrate this specific focus of price relationship into their trading psyches at all times, the better the ultimate result of their market actions.

CHAPTER 2

Overcoming the Psychological Barriers That Hold Most Spread Traders Back

A variety of psychological barriers hold traders back. To have a positive result in the market, it is imperative to understand how addressing each of these issues, individually, will optimize trading performance.

Essential Psychological Barriers to Successful Spread Trading

- Not defining a loss
- Not taking a loss or a profit
- Getting locked into a belief
- Getting "Boston-strangled"
- Kamikaze trading
- Euphoric trading
- Hesitating at your numbers
- Not catching a breakout
- Not focusing on opportunities

- Being more invested in being right than in making money
- Not consistently applying your trading system
- Not having a well-defined money management program
- Not being in the right state of mind

Let's review these barriers and discuss the ways in which each can get in the way of successful spread trading.

Not Defining a Loss

No one enters a trade assuming it will result in a loss. No one buys expecting the market to have topped out; conversely, no one sells expecting the market to rally to new highs. However, this occurs all too often. So upon entering any market, it is important that you have your downside defined, not after you enter a trade but before! If you are afraid to take a loss, don't trade. If you are long corn and short wheat, you must know where you are right and where you are wrong!

Not Taking a Loss or a Profit

There is an old trading axiom, "Your first loss is the best loss." It's true. Losing is an integral part of the process. So is the opposite, taking profits. If the market has reached your objective, don't be afraid to ring the register. Many times the market will not give you a second chance.

Getting Locked into a Belief

That is exactly what it is—prison. As George Segal succinctly put it, "The market is the boss." Your belief that silver is going to the moon or the dollar is going to hell in a handbasket is irrelevant. The market tells you everything! Listen! Remember what

Yogi Berra said, "You can observe a lot by just watching." It is important not to get locked into a belief that, just because gold is going down, the silver must follow.

Getting "Boston-Strangled"

There is an old Henny Youngman joke that was popular in the early 1960s, when the Boston strangler was not yet in police custody. A man is sitting in his living room, reading the evening newspaper and he hears a knock at the front door. Walking up to the door but not opening it he asks, "Who is it?"

The visitor answers, "It's the Boston strangler."

The man walks back into the apartment, passes the living room and into the kitchen, turns to his wife and says, "It's for you, dear!"

I always relate this anecdote at trading seminars as an analogy to taking a trade, over which you have no control, from someone else. In other words, a tip is like getting Boston-strangled. Don't do it! This is one door you don't want to open!

Kamikaze Trading

This means you're trading like a kamikaze pilot on his 44th mission. Perhaps you're feeling betrayed, angry; you need revenge. Snap out of it! You're going to crash-land.

Euphoric Trading

This is the opposite of kamikaze trading. You're feeling absolutely invincible, heroic, untouchable. Look out!

Hesitating at Your Numbers

You've done all this work—daily, weekly, and monthly charts. You've studied Gann, Fibonacci, Wyckoff, and Elliott waves. The market comes right down to your number, line, area, but you can't buy it!

Not Catching a Breakout

It's like going to the airport and watching the planes take off. Wouldn't it be fun just once to be on board and arrive at an exciting destination?

Not Focusing on Opportunities

For the spread trader, there are so many potential distractions in the market. How do you keep your focus clear, laser-straight? How do you get beyond all the head fakes?

Being More Invested in Being Right
Than in Making Money

In almost every trading room throughout the world, there are people who run around announcing to their colleagues that they have the high/low of every move in almost every market. What they don't possess are profits. The name of the game is making money. And yes, it's only a game!

Not Consistently Applying Your Trading System

If it's any good, you have to use it consistently. As the saying goes, "Use it or lose it."

Not Having a Well-Defined Money Management Program

You have heard this one many times before: "But the trade looked so good, so right." The object of money management is preservation of capital.

Not Being in the Right State of Mind

In my experience, over 80 percent of all trading failure is the result of not being in the right state of mind. The right state of mind produces the right results. As Gene Agatstein observed, "You get exactly the results you want. You produce your own success."

Successful trading then, in essence, comes down to this: overcoming your personal psychological barriers and conditioning yourself to produce feelings of self-trust, high self-esteem, unshakable conviction, and confidence, which naturally will lead to good judgment and winning trades based on a proven methodology.

CHAPTER 3

Strategy and the Overall Game Plan

The Essential Elements of a Successful Spread-Trading Strategy

- Assumes personal responsibility for all market actions
- Takes into consideration your motivation for trading
- Allows you to trade to win
- Establishes goals and formulates a plan to take action
- Controls anxiety
- Creates a point of focus
- Is consistent and congruent with your personality
- Allows you to have an edge
- Is automatic, effortless, and decisive in its implementation
- Manages risk and assumes losses
- Allows for patience and trading in a resourceful state of mind
- Is profit-oriented and practical, not theoretical
- Leaves no uncertainty
- Allows you to produce consistent results

- Identifies opportunities

Let's review these elements to see how they can directly impact the success of your spread-trading strategy.

Assumes Personal Responsibility for All Market Actions

It isn't your broker, your brother-in-law, the chairman of the board of the Fed, the fill, the computer, the unemployment report—it is you! It's a simple fact that must be understood in the adoption of any trading strategy: You produce the results. Good or bad, the buck stops here! The Nordstrom Corporation Policy Manual has just one sentence in it: "Use your own best judgment at all times."

Takes into Consideration Your Motivation for Trading

Your trading strategy must reflect your motive for trading. If you like the excitement of being in the market, perhaps you should consider not investing in software that takes four trades a year! It is important that your market behavior is consistent with your motive and motivation for trading.

Allows You to Trade to Win

Most traders don't trade to win, they trade not to lose. An effective strategy adopts a proactive market behavior that allows you to play full out; to buy aggressively at your numbers; to catch breakouts; to enter and exit at your signals. And yes, to win you have to risk loss.

Establishes Goals and Formulates a Plan to Take Action

Long- and short-range goals must be built into your strategy. What are you trying to accomplish today? This week? This month? This year? In addition, what specific plan can you adopt right now to achieve this goal in terms of outcome, performance, and motivation? Yes, there is a lot to think about!

Controls Anxiety

We have to deal with a variety of anxieties at all times when we are trading. A well-planned strategy minimizes anxiety by addressing factors that inevitably produce those feelings (e.g., loss, risk control, market reentry).

Creates a Point of Focus

The problem with most trading strategies is that in the final analysis there is no point of focus. You must know what you're looking for and what you're looking at. You must be able to distinguish the signal from the noise, winning from losing trades, high-probability from low-probability outcomes. The spread trader must always think in terms of the differential.

Is Consistent and Congruent with Your Personality

How many times have we been consulted by traders who have told us their strategy or system just doesn't "feel right," "look right," or "sound right"? Too often!

Allows You to Have an Edge

Unfortunately no "edge" is sold at the local department store, ready-made, one size fits all. It is just one more paradox of trading that in order to trade successfully you need an edge, but someone else's edge will do you no good. The saying, "one man's sugar is another man's salt" also applies to edge. You have to find your own and this fact is essential to having a winning strategy!

Is Automatic, Effortless, and Decisive in Its Implementation

Remember: "He who hesitates is lost."

Manages Risks and Assumes Losses

A good spread-trading strategy has the inevitability of loss built into it, so when you lose it is assumed to be inevitable and not unusual. Risk management assumes that no single loss will ever get out of hand. As in baseball, hitting safely three out of ten times can pay off very handsomely. Your strategy must inform you with certainty when you're wrong.

Allows for Patience and Trading in a Resourceful State of Mind

Once the trade is made, your strategy must allow you to remain calm, patient, and focused by presenting you with criteria of an objective (they're really all subjective) nature. You must work out, in your own mind, the contingency plans for dealing with a variety of market scenarios. Anything less is gambling!

Is Profit-Oriented and Practical, Not Theoretical

This point may seem obvious, although in reality it's not. Many spread traders develop strategies to be consistent with a particular ideological or technical bias rather than to make money. The name of the game is performance! Winston Churchill said, "It is a socialist idea that making profits is a vice; I consider the real vice is making losses." This is a point to be remembered in trading as well.

Leaves No Uncertainty

Think in probabilities; trade in certainties. Your strategy must allow you to know!

Allows You to Produce Consistent Results

Your strategy provides the organization and order to allow you to be consistent. The rest is up to you!

Identifies Opportunities

According to Anthony Robbins, "The difference between those who succeed and those who fail isn't what they have—it's what they choose to see and do with their resources and their experiences of life." This also applies to trading. Your trading strategy should allow you to open your eyes and see market opportunities so that you can act!

The Recipe for Spread-Trading Success

In *The Day Trader's Advantage*, I discussed the trading recipe for top-performing day traders; the same is applicable for spread trading.

- Identify market signals (e.g., spread entry point).
- React automatically with confidence and self-trust.
- Feel "good" or confident about the trade.

Technical Considerations

The specific technical system or approach that is utilized for spread trading must allow for the realization of these three conditions by providing the following:

- Market position and/or trend identification—Is the market in an uptrend, downtrend, or trading range?
- Automatic entry and exit—Where do I get in? Where do I get out?
- Defined money management—How much do I invest when the market doesn't share my enthusiasm for my position or appreciate my point of view?

In this section, I have provided what I believe to be the essential psychological and strategic considerations that must be consistently addressed for successful spread treading. In the following section, I will discuss in depth these technical factors:

- How does one analyze spread relationships from a purely technical vantage point?
- What is the most effective method of spread trading?
- How does one exploit seasonal and cyclical opportunities in the market?
- What is the most effective method of money management of spreads?

P·A·R·T

II

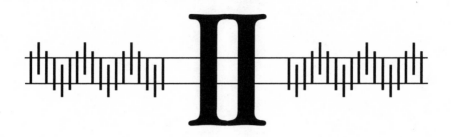

Technical Analysis
and
Spread Trading

CHAPTER 4

Market Analysis and Spread Trading

Spread trading, straddles, switches, pairs trading, arbitrage, and hedging have all melded to mean the same thing. With the exception of hedging, I will use the term *spreads* or *spread trading* to mean the simultaneous purchase of one market, month of a market, or security, and the sale of another market, month of a market, or security. *Hedging* refers to the simultaneous purchase or sale of a cash commodity, index, or financial instrument and a derivative of that cash (e.g., futures or options).

Many traders attempt to "spread up" or hedge an outright position, which is usually an attempt to avoid realizing a loss. This generally is a bad idea and is not part of any spreading technique in this book. My focus is on a strategy that treats a spread as a vehicle for profiting on the changes in the price relationship between two entities. The basis for the changes in the price difference between two markets could be fundamental, as in short-term supply shortages versus longer-term availability; seasonal, as in heating oil usage in the fall and winter versus the summer months; or cyclical, as in the difference between the live hogs and the live cattle supply cycle. There are many other obvious and not-so-obvious relationships. With the research support of Moore Research Center, Inc., a leading research firm in spreads, seasonals, and cycles, I will be able to introduce you to many old and new ideas that show remarkable statistical reliability over time.

Even as spread traders arm themselves with fundamental, seasonal, or cyclical information, it will still depend on the technical trading tools to increase their opportunities for success. The necessary technical ingredients for a successful approach to spread trading are trend identification, market entry, market exit, and money management.

Spread trading is trend trading. Although day trading or scalping a spread is possible, it is best left to the floor traders. Our spread opportunities will occur most often between three- and ten-day market swings and trends that may develop over weeks at a time. I personally use many of the trend-identifying techniques developed for swing and position trading for my spread trading methodology.

Being without a plan of action, that is, without knowing where the market is in relation to where it has been, increases the tendency of reaction to the emotion of the market and getting caught up in the crowd. In simple terms, this running with the herd often results in buying the highs and selling the lows—a common, painful experience!

Efficient market entry goes a long way to help prevent missing markets, eating into your profits, or widening a loss. Planning your entry and sticking to that plan will put you into the market when your emotions tell you to hesitate. Preparing for one or more contingencies will pace you in the market on your terms, not the market's.

One of the fatal flaws many traders make is to relax their money management criteria because they are trading a spread. Spreads can and do have large moves that can surprise the unwary.

It cannot be said too often or too loudly that the approach to successful spread trading has to be the same as the approach to successful outright trading. Many traders, to their regret, feel that they can treat spread trading differently or even casually. This is a major error in judgment.

Following are some personal axioms that I have found to help maintain a trading edge.

Patience

Capturing profits from relatively smaller price movements of two markets requires a bit more precision than trend following or swing trading. Carelessness will never be rewarded and neither will impatience. Patience is a trader's edge. Having an informed expectation about what the market will do and waiting patiently for the market to come to you gives you that edge.

High-Percentage Trades

High technology and sophisticated software have made it easier to track the intraday movement of spreads. However, the most successful traders still take their cue from openings and, most importantly, closes. High percentage spread trades will present themselves with fewer variables than will outright trades.

Anticipation of Market Opportunities Is Critical

Anticipation of potential market opportunities will help maximize trading results by giving the trader an earlier entry point or, if a move has already been established, by preparing the trader for the lowest risk entry.

Predetermined Buy and Sell Areas Must Be Executed

Many traders miss the market or have difficulty "pulling the trigger" because they have not prepared themselves to take advantage of the opportunities as they present themselves. Resting orders for entry and profit objectives go a long way to get you into the trade.

Trade One Setup Trade Per Market

It is a rare trader who is successful at reversing a market position because the market does not meet his or her immediate expectation. If the market does not perform as you anticipate, do not allow the emotions generated by the market make you chase after it. Stand back and determine if the market has really changed direction or the timing is wrong.

Ignore the Noise; Follow the Signal

Noise is market action without meaning. And much of the daily spread movement can fit into this category. The signal is the cue that put you into the market and it should be a related signal that takes you out of the market. Micromanaging a spread position will be a self-defeating chore.

Avoid Dull or Nonperforming Markets

If you have entered a dull or quiet market, it may be a better idea to stand aside and wait for the market to wake up and declare itself. Focusing on such quiet markets can drain your energy and take your attention away from more immediate opportunities.

The Innergame Spread-Trading Approach

The Innergame spread trading approach is based on three categories of market awareness: (1) the type of spread relationship (e.g., seasonal or cyclical), (2) the computer, and (3) the chart.

Spread Relationships

Traders must be aware of the kind of spread relationships they are trading even if they are using a totally technical trading method. Even the technical trader should have some background understanding of the fundamental, seasonal, or cyclical basis of the spread. Following are some examples:

Yield curve. Typically, when interest rates move, bonds, which represent the long end of the curve, lead the way as the big, sophisticated money moves there first. Trading the NOB (notes over bonds), or the MOB (municipals over bonds) is an interesting method to play the directional bias of the yield curve. (See Figures 4.1 and 4.2.)

Forex. Currency cross-trading is as old as money itself. Interest rates, balance of payments, political upheaval and other considerations lead to large, consistent price movements. (See Figures 4.3–4.6.)

Petroleum complex. Opportunities abound based on weather, supplies, season, politics, and economic conditions, to name a few factors that might affect this complex. For example, demand for winter-delivery heating oil gradually builds into the fall in preparation for cold weather. (See Figure 4.7.) The summer months offer dynamic markets as well, with the petroleum products taking turns leading prices, but with bull spreads favored for all three markets. (See Figures 4.8–4.12.)

Grains and soy complex. This category offers an abundance of possibilities for spreading intermarket, intramarket, interexchange. and of course the crush (soybeans versus soy meal and soybean oil). It should be noted that, although there is a very strong seasonal rationale for most of the popular spread strategies, there are years when abnormal price movements occur because of weather, supply dislocation, disease, or politics. One thing seems to remain the same and that is a very popular and heavily used spread market in most of the grain complex. (See Figures 4.13–4.24.)

Livestock complex. Breeding, weather, economics, and politics all play a role in moving the spread relationships in this complex. According to Jerry Toepke of the Moore Research Center, Inc., "Because of the consistency in breeding (required by weather considerations), one of the more reliable seasonal moves over the years has been the rise in live cattle prices from fall into spring. As one might expect, then, bull spreads have also tended to be consistent during fall."

As of the February 1997 futures contract, the Chicago Mercantile Exchange has replaced the live hog contract with one for lean hogs. Although the lean-hog contract is new, I have, with the help of Moore Research Center, Inc. included several historical spread charts for your consideration. All values reflect historical live-hog prices converted to lean-hog equivalents. (See Figures 4.28–4.32.)

Livestock markets can be as dynamic as grains in their interrelationships. Feeder cattle, live cattle, and hogs are being buffeted by the huge price movements in the grain complex and therefore are creating more opportunities for profit. (See Figures 4.25–4.32.)

Softs. The softs include cocoa, sugar, orange juice, coffee, and cotton. Although most of the spread activity in this category is intramarket, very strong and interesting opportunities present themselves continually. (See Figures 4.33–4.38.)

Computer Setup

There are several ways to use the computer and its power in spread trading. Moore Research Center, Inc., publishes years of data that show high-probability spread relationships in dozens of markets.

Many of the same computer-generated formulas that are used in trading outright positions will work just as well for spread prices. This is especially true of any trend-identifying method that a computer supplies to you. I use just a few proprietary computer–generated numbers. There is a trend identifier, a momentum oscillator, and a pivot that is derived from the momentum oscillator. (See Figure 4.39.) It is in this category that you can utilize your imagination to find the best approach available to you. One common error, in my view, that many traders make is to rely on this tool to the exclusion of either the fundamental setup or our next category, which I call chart setup.

Chart Setup

Classical chart analysis and the simple chart are perfect media for analyzing technical elements of a spread, using the simplest ideas of classical charting such as the following:

- Trend and pattern recognition
- Natural market retracements
- Highs and lows

Trend and pattern recognition. For me, the overriding concept is the KISS method of trading. Keeping it simple works and it works especially well for spread trading. Trendlines, moving averages, fractals, and so on, are all designed to identify a trend and signal its end. (See Figure 4.40.) The patterns that a spread chart will show are similar to those of any other chart you might be using. (See Figure 4.41.) Signals from those patterns have the same reliability as do those for outright markets.

Natural market retracements. Support and resistance areas, Fibonacci ratios, Gann lines, Elliott waves, and so on, methods commonly used to quantify market retracements, are perfectly valid for spread trading.

Highs and lows. Previous highs and lows have the same significance in spread trading as they do in outright trading. (See Figure 4.42.)

Creating a Road Map for Trades

Carefully thought-out preparation and planning in order to be able to anticipate market action can be effective only if traders are consistent with the various elements of their methodology. The important landmarks on your road map are the trend of the market, any patterns, previous highs and lows, and any computer-generated numbers.

Trend

The simplest definition of a trend is a series of higher highs and higher lows or a series of lower highs and lower lows that gives us an opportunity to create a very simple trading device. A trend is in force each time the market makes a new high after completing a retracement. (See Figure 4.43.) As long as this continues to be true, we can say the market is still in its trend. For spread trading, I believe in Newton's third law—a body in motion tends to stay in motion. You get the idea. Trendlines, moving averages, and channel breakouts are all important methods in identifying a spread trend. (See Figure 4.44.) My computer-generated trend identifier shown in Figure 4.45 is another tool, but a tool used only in conjunction with other information.

Pattern recognition. This landmark includes the old standby patterns such as triangles, flag patterns, double and triple tops and bottoms, constricted ranges, and others similar to those seen in outright trading. (See Figure 4.46.)

Computer-generated numbers. Most traders have a library of useful and proven computer numbers. They may be applied with success in spread trading. The only caveat, however, is that they usually are not self-contained systems and should be used along with the several other devices I have spoken about.

Putting It All Together

After hundreds of interviews, close personal relationships with some of the country's best traders, and my personal market experiences, I have learned this: there is not a consistently profitable trader who hasn't prepared rigorously for trading. The most important part of your preparation must be preparing yourself emotionally, psychologically and physically to be resourceful, disciplined, and committed to whatever the market throws your way.

Remember, it all comes down to these three things:

1. Identifying an opportunity
2. Taking action automatically
3. Feeling good about the trade

Identifying an Opportunity

You have invested your valuable time and effort. You have created a set of reasonable tools with which to operate in the market. Now you must be prepared to act!

Taking Action Automatically

You must be disciplined and consistent in acting on your ideas. Each time that the market does what you anticipated will reinforce your discipline and feeling of trading confidence.

Feeling Good about the Trade

Every trade you make that is made according to the guidelines you have designed, whether a profit or loss, is a good trade. Trading is a process, and success is measured after many trades in that process. You must always operate from this market attitude.

FIGURE 4.1

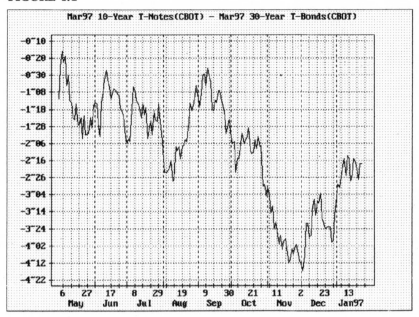

FIGURE 4.2

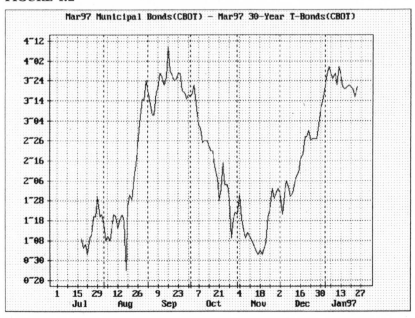

FIGURE 4.3

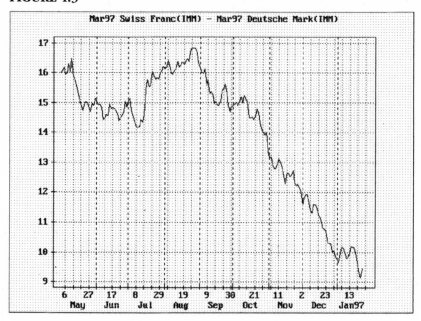

FIGURE 4.4

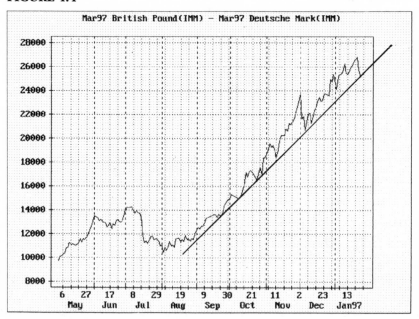

FIGURE 4.5

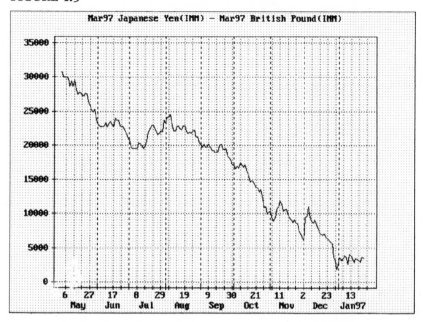

FIGURE 4.6

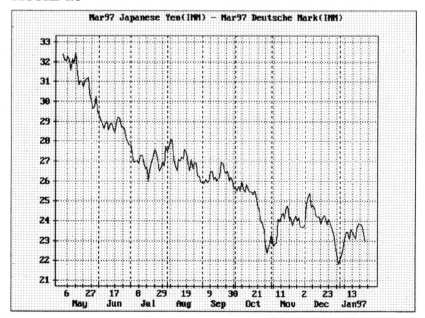

FIGURE 4.7

FIGURE 4.8

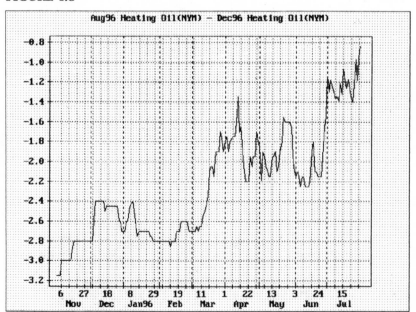

FIGURE 4.9

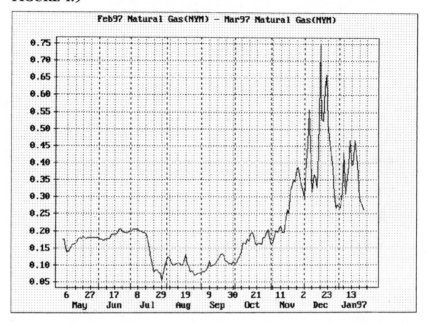

FIGURE 4.10

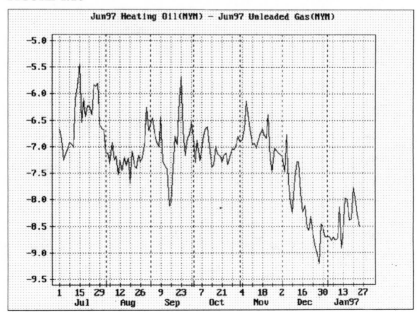

FIGURE 4.11

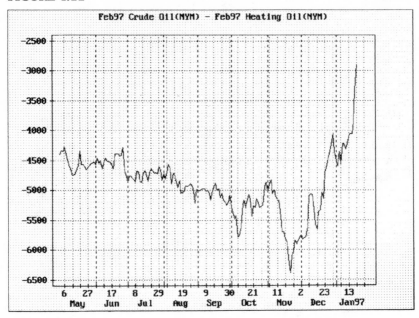

FIGURE 4.12

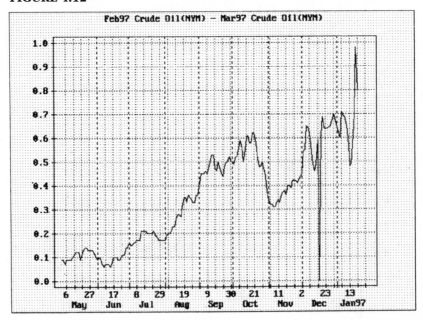

FIGURE 4.13

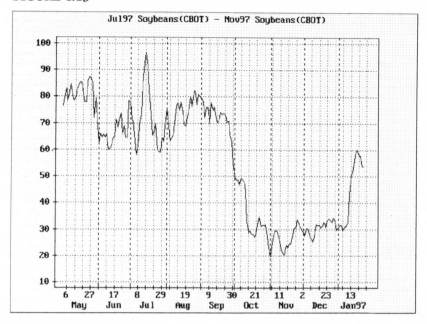

FIGURE 4.14

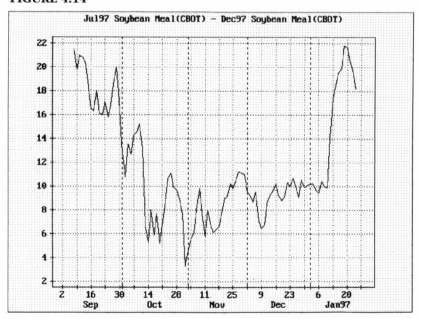

FIGURE 4.15

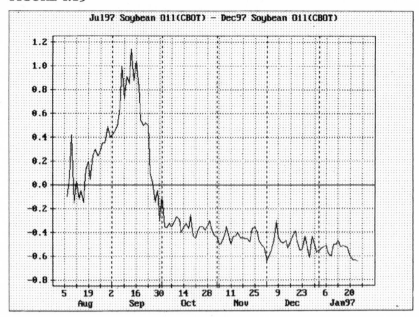

FIGURE 4.16

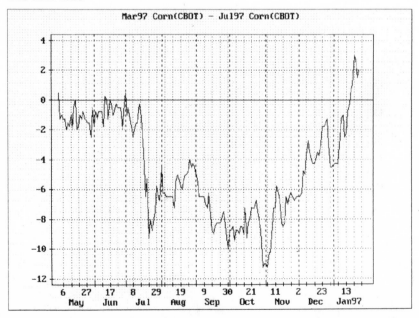

FIGURE 4.17

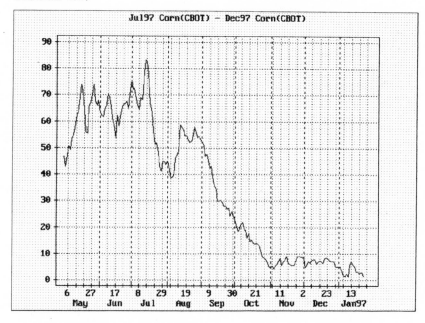

FIGURE 4.18

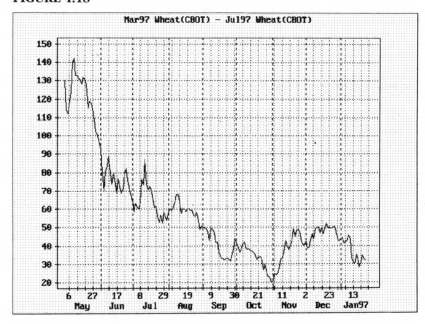

FIGURE 4.19

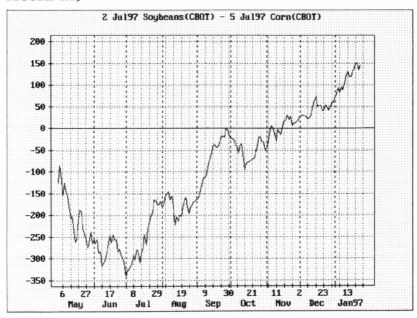

FIGURE 4.20

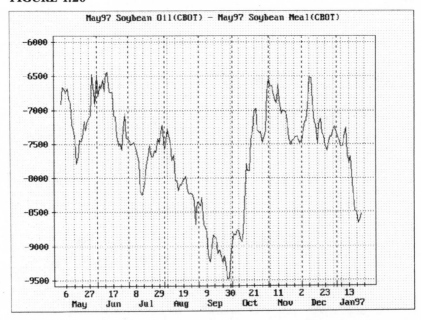

FIGURE 4.21

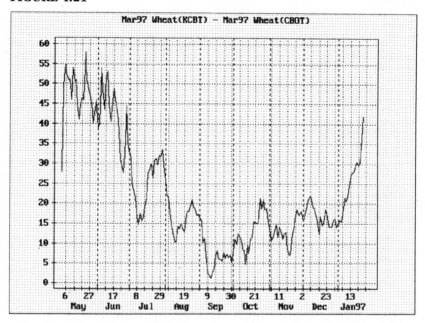

Mar97 Wheat(KCBT) — Mar97 Wheat(CBOT)

FIGURE 4.22

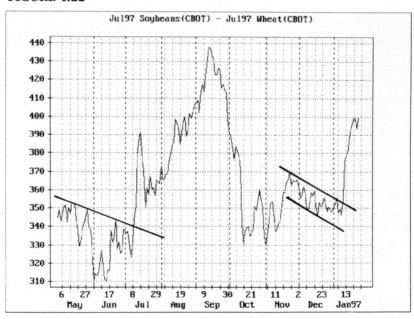

Jul97 Soybeans(CBOT) — Jul97 Wheat(CBOT)

FIGURE 4.23

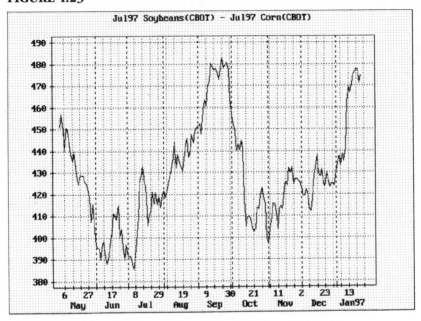

FIGURE 4.24

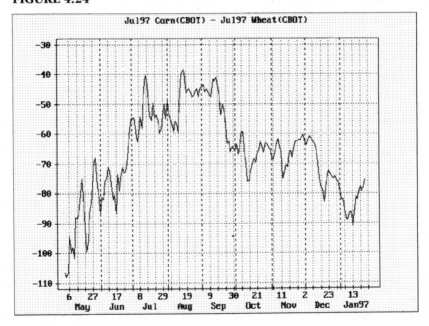

FIGURE 4.25

FIGURE 4.26

FIGURE 4.27

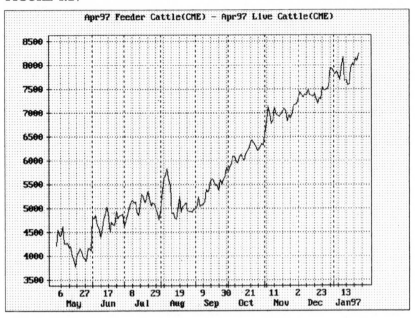

FIGURE 4.28

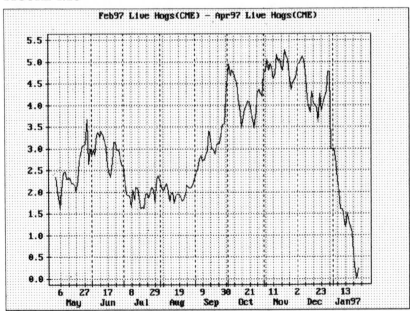

FIGURE 4.29

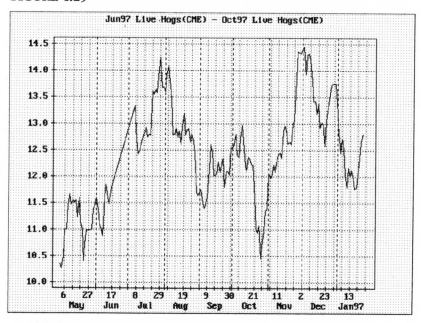

FIGURE 4.30

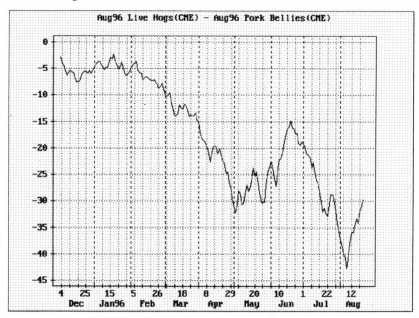

FIGURE 4.31

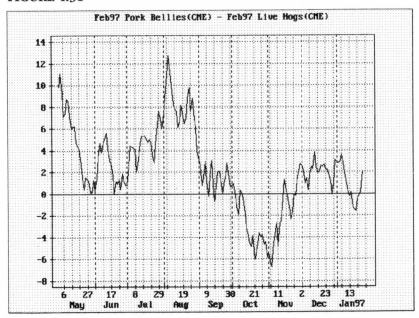

FIGURE 4.32

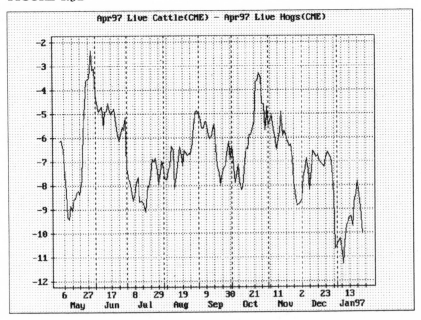

FIGURE 4.33

FIGURE 4.34

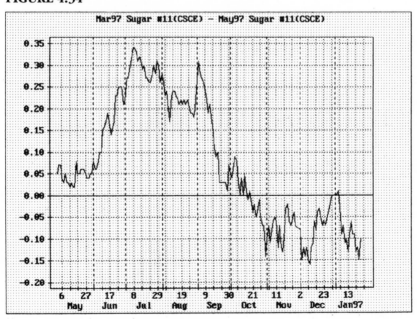

FIGURE 4.35

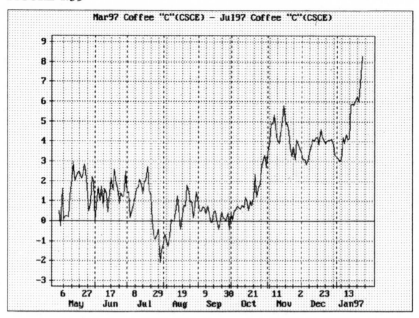

FIGURE 4.36

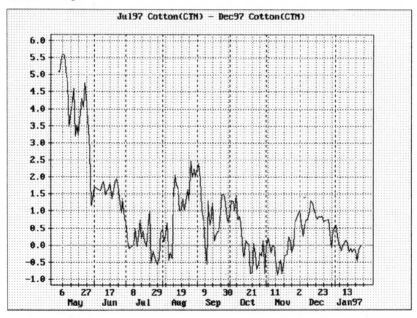

FIGURE 4.37

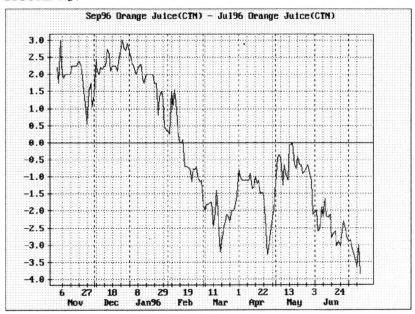

FIGURE 4.38

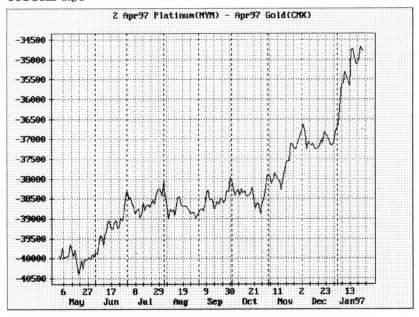

FIGURE 4.39

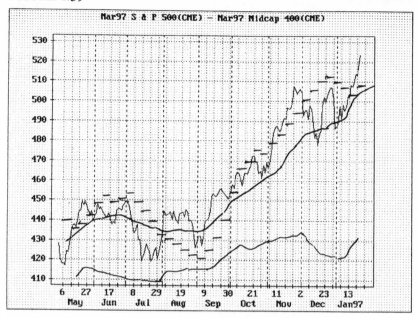

FIGURE 4.40

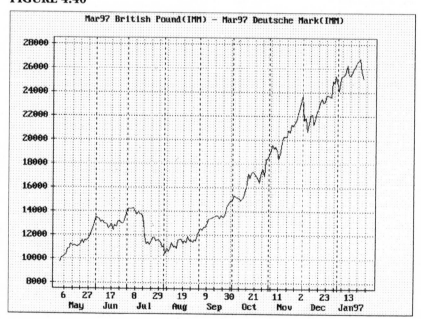

FIGURE 4.41

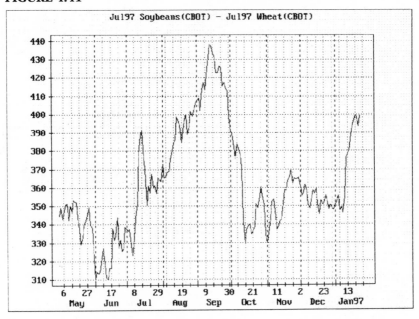

FIGURE 4.42

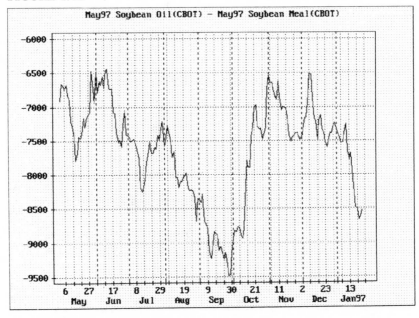

FIGURE 4.43

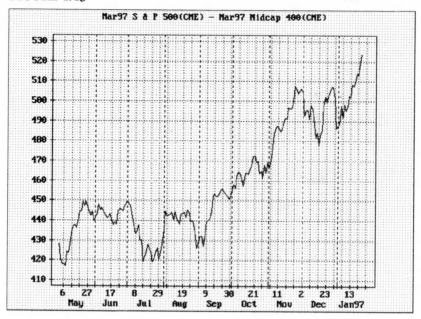

FIGURE 4.44

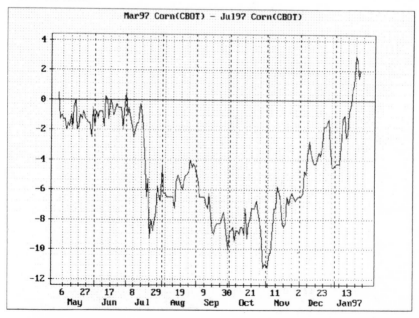

FIGURE 4.45

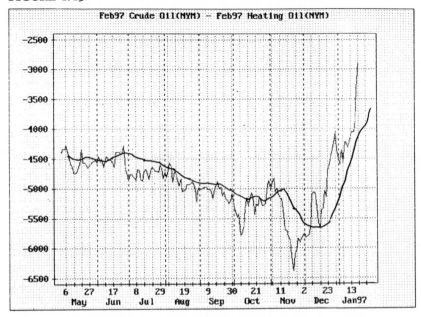

FIGURE 4.46

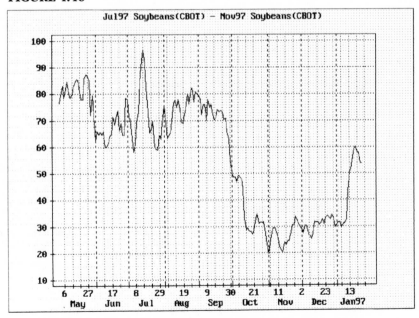

Seasonal, Cyclical, and Historical Spread Relationships

The following tables are listings of seasonal, cyclical, and historical spread trades that have been researched by Moore Research Center, Inc. The spread strategies included here do not constitute buy or sell recommendations; rather they are quantified historical fact. Ideally, these trading ideas should be entered only with the assistance of fundamental and/or technical analysis, for instance, with indicators that confirm seasonal movement or timing signals that trigger entry.

Some listings may be similar to others but illustrate a longer or shorter trade window. Others may be coincident with first delivery and should be approached accordingly. Sound money management principles should always prevail in any spread strategy.

The spread tables are presented in a one-year cycle beginning with January 1996 and ending with December 1996. After each monthly table, one specific spread trade is highlighted to demonstrate what each spread would look like over a 15-year period. Additionally, a table and chart are presented at the end of this chapter to reveal the history of the "January effect" going back to 1983.

January Spreads

Futures Trade	Entry Date	Exit Date	Win Pct	Win Years	Loss Years	Total Years	Average Profit	Avg Pft Per Day
Buy May Soybean Oil(CBT)- BOK[6] Sell May Soybean Meal(CBT)- SMK[6]	1/4	2/20	93	14	1	15	663	14.10
Buy Mar Unleaded Gas(NYM)- HUH[6] Sell Mar Heating Oil(NYM)- HOH[6]	1/8	2/4	80	8	2	10	872	32.28
Buy Jul Wheat(CBT)- WN[6] Sell May Wheat(CBT)- WK[6]	1/9	2/19	100	15	0	15	437	10.65
Buy Nov Soybeans(CBT)- SX[6] Sell May Soybeans(CBT)- SK[6]	1/10	1/29	100	15	0	15	694	36.54
Buy Jul Wheat(KCBT)- KWN[6] Sell Jul Soybeans(CBT)- SN[6]	1/10	2/9	87	13	2	15	1066	35.53
Buy Apr Live Cattle(CME)- LCJ[6] Sell Apr Feeder Cattle(CME)- FCJ[6]	1/10	3/27	100	15	0	15	1026	13.33
Buy Mar Silver(CMX)- SIH[6] Sell Apr Gold(CMX)- GCJ[6]	1/11	2/15	93	14	1	15	1443	41.22
Buy May Heating Oil(NYM)- HOK[6] Sell Mar Heating Oil(NYM)- HOH[6]	1/14	1/24	80	12	3	15	422	42.17
Buy Mar Eurodollars(IMM)- EDH[6] Sell Mar 3-Mth T-Bills(IMM)- TBH[6]	1/14	2/8	92	12	1	13	381	15.23
Buy Apr Live Cattle(CME)- LCJ[6] Sell Aug Live Cattle(CME)- LCQ[6]	1/24	3/1	93	14	1	15	463	12.53

Moore Research Center, Inc.

Buy Mar Deutsche Mark(IMM)- DMH[6] Sell Mar Swiss Franc(IMM)- SFH[6]	1/25	2/12	93	14	1	15	733	40.69
Buy Apr Live Cattle(CME)- LCJ[6] Sell Apr Live Hogs(CME)- LHJ[6]	1/25	2/24	93	14	1	15	1087	36.23
Buy Mar Japanese Yen(IMM)- JYH[6] Sell Mar Swiss Franc(IMM)- SFH[6]	1/28	2/15	93	14	1	15	1879	104.40
Buy Mar Value-Line(KCBT)- KVH[6] Sell Mar NYSE Composite(NYFE)- YXH[6]	1/28	2/15	92	12	1	13	2104	116.88
Buy Jun Live Hogs(CME)- LHM[6] Sell Jul Pork Bellies(CME)- PBN[6]	1/30	2/29	100	15	0	15	1017	33.88

Note: One column in the above table equates each trade by its *impact* or daily return. Ave Pft Per Day quantifies the average historical profit (including losses) per day of trade maintenance, i.e., historical daily return.

Moore Research Center, Inc.

Buy Mar 96 D-Mark(IMM) / Sell Mar 96 Swiss Franc(IMM)

Enter on approximately 01/25 - Exit on approximately 02/12

CONT YEAR	ENTRY DATE	ENTRY PRICE	EXIT DATE	EXIT PRICE	PROFIT	PROFIT AMOUNT	PEAK EQUITY DATE	PEAK EQUITY AMOUNT	WORST DRAWDOWN DATE	WORST DRAWDOWN AMOUNT
1995	01/25/95	-12.58	02/10/95	-12.27	0.31	387.50	02/07/95	925.00	01/27/95	-12.50
1994	01/25/94	-11.15	02/11/94	-10.61	0.54	675.00	02/11/94	675.00	02/03/94	-537.50
1993	01/25/93	-5.93	02/12/93	-4.74	1.19	1487.50	02/12/93	1487.50		
1992	01/27/92	-7.97	02/12/92	-7.33	0.64	800.00	02/12/92	800.00		
1991	01/25/91	-12.13	02/12/91	-11.52	0.61	762.50	02/12/91	762.50	02/06/91	-37.50
1990	01/25/90	-7.81	02/12/90	-6.86	0.95	1187.50	02/07/90	1337.50		
1989	01/25/89	-9.68	02/10/89	-9.49	0.19	237.50	01/31/89	487.50	02/09/89	-37.50
1988	01/25/88	-14.13	02/12/88	-12.74	1.39	1737.50	02/12/88	1737.50	01/26/88	-50.00
1987	01/26/87	-10.50	02/12/87	-9.98	0.52	650.00	02/12/87	650.00	01/28/87	-325.00
1986	01/27/86	-7.55	02/12/86	-8.67	-1.12	-1400.00	02/03/86	12.50	02/12/86	-1400.00
1985	01/25/85	-6.01	02/12/85	-5.41	0.60	750.00	02/08/85	837.50	01/29/85	-12.50
1984	01/25/84	-9.36	02/10/84	-8.50	0.86	1075.00	02/09/84	1087.50		
1983	01/25/83	-9.25	02/11/83	-8.55	0.70	875.00	02/10/83	1362.50	01/28/83	-150.00
1982	01/25/82	-10.87	02/12/82	-10.43	0.44	550.00	02/09/82	612.50	01/29/82	-600.00
1981	01/26/81	-5.57	02/12/81	-4.60	0.97	1212.50	02/12/81	1212.50		

Percentage Correct	93		Protective Stop	(952)
Average Profit on Winning Trades	0.71	884.82	Winners	14
Average Loss on Trades	-1.12	-1400.00	Losers	1
Average Net Profit Per Trade	0.59	732.50	Total trades	15

February Spreads

Moore Research Center, Inc.

Futures Trade	Entry Date	Exit Date	Win Pct	Win Years	Loss Years	Total Years	Average Profit	Avg Pft Per Day
Buy Apr Live Cattle(CME)- LCJ^6 / Sell Aug Live Cattle(CME)- LCQ^6	2/1	3/5	93	14	1	15	488	14.78
Buy Jul Cotton(CTN)- CTN^6 / Sell Dec Cotton(CTN)- CTZ^6	2/2	2/28	87	13	2	15	1003	38.59
Buy Mar Wheat(KCBT)- KWH^6 / Sell Mar Wheat(CBT)- WH^6	2/2	2/28	80	12	3	15	486	18.69
Buy Jul Unleaded Gas(NYM)- HUN^6 / Sell Apr Unleaded Gas(NYM)- HUJ^6	2/6	3/8	90	9	1	10	522	16.84
Buy Apr Live Cattle(CME)- LCJ^6 / Sell Mar Feeder Cattle(CME)- FCH^6	2/9	3/10	100	15	0	15	761	25.37
Buy Jul Corn(CBT)- CN^6 / Sell Jul Wheat(CBT)- WN^6	2/10	3/25	87	13	2	15	545	12.39
Buy Jun Live Hogs(CME)- LHM^6 / Sell Oct Live Hogs(CME)- LHV^6	2/12	3/8	93	14	1	15	430	17.18
Buy May Unleaded Gas(NYM)- HUK^6 / Sell May Heating Oil(NYM)- HOK^6	2/13	3/30	90	9	1	10	845	18.36
Buy Jul Soybeans(CBT)- SN^6 / Sell Jul Wheat(CBT)- WN^6	2/13	3/31	93	14	1	15	1023	21.77
Buy Nov Soybeans(CBT)- SX^6 / Sell Dec Corn(CBT)- CZ^6	2/14	4/1	100	15	0	15	651	13.85

Buy Jun 30-Year T-Bonds(CBT)- USM[6] Sell Jun Municipal Bonds(CBT)- MBM[6]	2/18	3/28	90	9	1	10	1378	35.34
Buy Jun Deutsche Mark(IMM)- DMM[6] Sell Jun Swiss Franc(IMM)- SFM[6]	2/21	3/25	87	13	2	15	473	14.34
Buy Jun Unleaded Gas(NYM)- HUM[6] Sell Jun Crude Oil(NYM)- CLM[6]	2/24	4/6	100	10	0	10	557	13.27
Buy Mar Value-Line(KCBT)- KVH[6] Sell Mar NYSE Composite(NYFE)- YXH[6]	2/25	3/4	100	13	0	13	1392	174.04
Buy Aug Live Hogs(CME)- LHQ[6] Sell Aug Live Cattle(CME)- LCQ[6]	2/27	4/18	93	14	1	15	768	15.06

Note: One column in the above table equates each trade by its *impact* or daily return. Ave Pft Per Day quantifies the average historical profit (including losses) per day of trade maintenance, i.e., historical daily return.

Buy Apr Live Cattle(CME) / Sell Aug Live Cattle(CME)

Moore Research Center, Inc.

Enter on approximately 02/01 - Exit on approximately 03/05

CONT YEAR	ENTRY DATE	ENTRY PRICE	EXIT DATE	EXIT PRICE	PROFIT	PROFIT AMOUNT	BEST EQUITY DATE	BEST EQUITY AMOUNT	WORST EQUITY DATE	WORST EQUITY AMOUNT
1995	02/01/95	9.32	03/06/95	10.02	0.70	280.00	03/03/95	392.00	02/22/95	-220.00
1994	02/01/94	2.60	03/04/94	3.95	1.35	540.00	03/04/94	540.00	02/04/94	-320.00
1993	02/01/93	6.63	03/05/93	9.23	2.60	1040.00	02/24/93	1076.00		
1992	02/03/92	8.50	03/05/92	8.80	0.30	120.00	02/07/92	280.00	02/24/92	-320.00
1991	02/01/91	3.90	03/06/91	6.35	2.45	980.00	03/06/91	980.00	02/08/91	-120.00
1990	02/01/90	5.15	03/06/90	5.63	0.48	192.00	02/12/90	560.00	02/28/90	-128.00
1989	02/01/89	3.30	03/06/89	5.23	1.93	772.00	02/27/89	920.00	02/10/89	-180.00
1988	02/01/88	3.68	03/04/88	4.42	0.74	296.00	02/22/88	688.00		
1987	02/02/87	3.90	03/06/87	5.13	1.23	492.00	02/23/87	880.00		
1986	02/03/86	2.05	03/06/86	2.93	0.88	352.00	02/26/86	628.00	02/18/86	-460.00
1985	02/01/85	2.10	03/06/85	-1.38	-3.48	-1392.00			03/04/85	-1492.00
1984	02/01/84	2.05	03/05/84	5.10	3.05	1220.00	03/05/84	1220.00	02/06/84	-60.00
1983	02/01/83	-0.93	03/04/83	1.60	2.53	1012.00	03/02/83	1140.00		
1982	02/01/82	1.27	03/05/82	4.78	3.51	1404.00	03/05/82	1404.00		
1981	02/02/81	-3.32	03/06/81	-3.30	0.02	8.00	02/06/81	268.00	02/20/81	-184.00
Percentage Correct	93									(634)
Average Profit on Winning Trades					1.56	622.00	Protective Stop		Winners	14
Average Loss on Trades					-3.48	-1392.00			Losers	1
Average Net Profit Per Trade					1.22	487.73			Total trades	15

March Spreads

Moore Research Center, Inc.

Futures Trade	Entry Date	Exit Date	Win Pct	Win Years	Loss Years	Total Years	Average Profit	Avg Pft Per Day
Buy Jul Soybeans(CBT)- SN[6] **Sell Jul Wheat(CBT)- WN[6]**	3/1	3/28	93	14	1	15	591	21.88
Buy Jun Heating Oil(NYM)- HOM[6] **Sell Sep Heating Oil(NYM)- HOU[6]**	3/1	4/24	87	13	2	15	428	7.93
Buy May Pork Bellies(CME)- PBK[6] **Sell Apr Live Hogs(CME)- LHJ[6]**	3/3	3/23	87	13	2	15	701	35.05
Buy Jun 30-Year T-Bonds(CBT)- USM[6] **Sell Jun Municipal Bonds(CBT)- MBM[6]**	3/3	3/29	90	9	1	10	681	26.20
Buy Jun Eurodollars(IMM)- EDM[6] **Sell Jun Eurodollars(IMM)- EDM[7]**	3/4	4/27	83	10	2	12	588	10.88
Buy Jun 10-Year T-Notes(CBT)- TYM[6] **Sell Jun Municipal Bonds(CBT)- MBM[6]**	3/6	4/2	90	9	1	10	634	23.50
Buy May Unleaded Gas(NYM)- HUK[6] **Sell May Heating Oil(NYM)- HOK[6]**	3/8	3/27	100	10	0	10	446	23.45
Buy Jun Unleaded Gas(NYM)- HUM[6] **Sell Sep Unleaded Gas(NYM)- HUU[6]**	3/20	4/27	90	9	1	10	806	21.21
Buy Apr Live Cattle(CME)- LCJ[6] **Sell Apr Live Hogs(CME)- LHJ[6]**	3/21	3/30	93	14	1	15	550	61.13
Buy May Unleaded Gas(NYM)- HUK[6] **Sell May Crude Oil(NYM)- CLK[6]**	3/21	3/31	90	9	1	10	630	62.99

Buy Jul Platinum(NYM)- PLN[6] Sell Jun Gold(CMX)- GCM[6]	3/21	5/3	87	13	2	15	732	17.02
Buy Jun Live Hogs(CME)- LHM[6] Sell Jul Pork Bellies(CME)- PBN[6]	3/23	5/24	93	14	1	15	1702	27.46
Buy Jun Japanese Yen(IMM)- JYM[6] Sell Jun Swiss Franc(IMM)- SFM[6]	3/29	5/4	93	14	1	15	1517	42.13
Buy Jun Live Hogs(CME)- LHM[6] Sell Jun Live Cattle(CME)- LCM[6]	3/30	5/23	93	14	1	15	1174	21.74
Buy Jun S & P 500(CME)- SPM[6] Sell Jun Value-Line(KCBT)- KVM[6]	3/31	4/21	93	13	1	14	1520	72.36

Note: One column in the above table equates each trade by its *impact* or daily return. Ave Pft Per Day quantifies the average historical profit (including losses) per day of trade maintenance, i.e., historical daily return.

Moore Research Center, Inc.

Buy May Unleaded Reg.(NYM) / Sell May Heating Oil #2(NYM)

Enter on approximately 03/08 - Exit on approximately 03/27

CONT YEAR	ENTRY DATE	ENTRY PRICE	EXIT DATE	EXIT PRICE	PROFIT	PROFIT AMOUNT	BEST EQUITY DATE	BEST EQUITY AMOUNT	WORST EQUITY DATE	WORST EQUITY AMOUNT
1995	03/08/95	9.59	03/27/95	10.40	0.81	340.20	03/24/95	554.40	03/10/95	-1029.00
1994	03/08/94	2.46	03/25/94	2.87	0.41	172.20	03/23/94	491.40		
1993	03/08/93	3.22	03/26/93	3.39	0.17	71.40	03/26/93	71.40	03/22/93	-575.40
1992	03/09/92	8.01	03/27/92	8.02	0.01	4.20	03/11/92	42.00	03/23/92	-550.20
1991	03/08/91	13.87	03/27/91	14.10	0.23	96.60	03/11/91	554.40	03/14/91	-541.80
1990	03/08/90	7.65	03/27/90	10.41	2.76	1159.20	03/26/90	1285.20	03/12/90	-197.40
1989	03/08/89	5.52	03/27/89	7.63	2.11	886.20	03/27/89	886.20	03/10/89	-138.60
1988	03/08/88	2.34	03/25/88	2.66	0.32	134.40	03/17/88	483.00	03/23/88	-96.60
1987	03/09/87	4.22	03/27/87	4.85	0.63	264.60	03/25/87	487.20		
1986	03/10/86	-1.47	03/27/86	1.69	3.16	1327.20	03/26/86	1419.60	03/11/86	-609.00
Percentage Correct	100						Protective Stop	(579)		
Average Profit on Winning Trades					1.06	445.62	Winners	10		
Average Loss on Trades							Losers	0		
Average Net Profit Per Trade					1.06	445.62	Total trades	10		

HYPOTHETICAL OR SIMULATED PERFORMANCE RESULTS HAVE CERTAIN INHERENT LIMITATIONS. UNLIKE AN ACTUAL PERFORMANCE RECORD, SIMULATED RESULTS DO NOT REPRESENT ACTUAL TRADING. ALSO, SINCE THE TRADES HAVE NOT ACTUALLY BEEN EXECUTED, THE RESULTS MAY HAVE UNDER-OR OVER-COMPENSATED FOR THE IMPACT, IF ANY, OF CERTAIN MARKET FACTORS, SUCH AS LACK OF LIQUIDITY. SIMULATED TRADING PROGRAMS IN GENERAL ARE ALSO SUBJECT TO THE FACT THAT THEY ARE DESIGNED WITH THE BENEFIT OF HINDSIGHT. NO REPRESENTATION IS BEING MADE THAT ANY ACCOUNT WILL OR IS LIKELY TO ACHIEVE PROFITS OR LOSSES SIMILAR TO THOSE SHOWN. SIMULATED RESULTS DO NOT NECESSARILY IMPLY FUTURE PROFITS. THE RISK OF LOSS IN TRADING COMMODITY CONTRACTS CAN BE SUBSTANTIAL. YOU SHOULD THEREFORE, CAREFULLY CONSIDER WHETHER SUCH TRADING IS SUITABLE FOR YOU IN LIGHT OF YOUR FINANCIAL CONDITION. RESULTS NOT ADJUSTED FOR COMMISSION AND SLIPPAGE.

April Spreads

Futures Trade	Entry Date	Exit Date	Win Pct	Win Years	Loss Years	Total Years	Average Profit	Avg Pft Per Day
Buy Jun Japanese Yen(IMM)- JYM[6] Sell Jun Deutsche Mark(IMM)- DMM[6]	4/1	4/22	93	14	1	15	1433	68.21
Buy Jun Japanese Yen(IMM)- JYM[6] Sell Jun Swiss Franc(IMM)- SFM[6]	4/1	5/5	93	14	1	15	1290	37.94
Buy Dec Soybean Oil(CBOT)- BOZ[6] Sell Dec Soybean Meal(CBOT)- SMZ[6]	4/2	5/22	80	12	3	15	610	12.20
Buy Jun S & P 500(CME)- SPM[6] Sell Jun NYSE Composite(NYFE)- YXM[6]	4/4	4/16	92	12	1	13	1177	98.08
Buy Jun Unleaded Gas(NYM)- HUM[6] Sell Oct Unleaded Gas(NYM)- HUV[6]	4/9	4/24	90	9	1	10	596	39.70
Buy Jul Unleaded Gas(NYM)- HUN[6] Sell Jul Heating Oil(NYM)- HON[6]	4/9	5/12	80	8	2	10	721	21.85
Buy Jun 10-Year T-Notes(CBOT)- TYM[6] Sell Jun 30-Year T-Bonds(CBOT)- USM[6]	4/11	4/23	92	12	1	13	591	49.28
Buy Jun Municipal Bonds(CBOT)- MBM[6] Sell Jun 30-Year T-Bonds(CBOT)- USM[6]	4/13	4/26	90	9	1	10	959	73.80
Buy Aug Live Hogs(CME)- LHQ[6] Sell Aug Live Cattle(CME)- LCQ[6]	4/14	5/20	93	14	1	15	834	23.16
Buy Aug Gold(CMX)- GCQ[6] Sell Sep Silver(CMX)- SIU[6]	4/16	6/27	80	12	3	15	1750	24.30

Moore Research Center, Inc.

Buy Jun Live Hogs(CME)- LHM[6] **Sell Jul Pork Bellies(CME)- PBN[6]**	4/26	5/27	93	14	1	15	1065	34.35
Buy Dec Cotton(CTN)- CTZ[6] **Sell Oct Cotton(CTN)- CTV[6]**	4/26	7/18	80	12	3	15	515	6.20
Buy Jul Corn(CBOT)- CN[6] **Sell Jul Wheat(CBOT)- WN[6]**	4/27	6/18	80	12	3	15	555	10.67

Note: One column in the above table equates each trade by its *impact* or daily return. <u>Ave Pft Per Day</u> quantifies the average historical profit (including losses) per day of trade maintenance, i.e., historical daily return.

Moore Research Center, Inc. — Buy Jun Live Hogs(CME) / Sell Jul Pork Bellies(CME)

Enter on approximately 04/26 - Exit on approximately 05/27

CONT YEAR	ENTRY DATE	ENTRY PRICE	EXIT DATE	EXIT PRICE	PROFIT	PROFIT AMOUNT	BEST EQUITY DATE	BEST EQUITY AMOUNT	WORST EQUITY DATE	WORST EQUITY AMOUNT
1995	04/26/95	4.53	05/26/95	6.22	1.69	676.00	05/17/95	776.00	05/02/95	-372.00
1994	04/26/94	-0.13	05/27/94	5.70	5.83	2332.00	05/26/94	2532.00		
1993	04/26/93	4.40	05/27/93	11.45	7.05	2820.00	05/27/93	2820.00		
1992	04/27/92	12.70	05/27/92	13.35	0.65	260.00	05/01/92	480.00	05/19/92	-1200.00
1991	04/29/91	-6.37	05/28/91	-1.25	5.12	2048.00	05/20/91	2908.00		
1990	04/27/90	-2.02	05/25/90	0.10	2.12	848.00	05/15/90	1260.00	05/03/90	-1472.00
1989	04/27/89	14.95	05/26/89	16.53	1.58	632.00	05/26/89	632.00	05/12/89	-1212.00
1988	04/26/88	-2.90	05/27/88	-0.70	2.20	880.00	05/19/88	1348.00	04/27/88	-228.00
1987	04/27/87	-18.85	05/28/87	-14.45	4.40	1760.00	05/22/87	3052.00	05/05/87	-392.00
1986	04/28/86	-11.42	05/28/86	-16.57	-5.15	-2060.00			05/14/86	-2312.00
1985	04/29/85	-21.02	05/28/85	-16.72	4.30	1720.00	05/13/85	2288.00		
1984	04/26/84	-12.27	05/25/84	-11.07	1.20	480.00	05/14/84	748.00	05/07/84	-812.00
1983	04/27/83	-16.62	05/27/83	-13.45	3.17	1268.00	05/25/83	1768.00	05/06/83	-624.00
1982	04/27/82	-24.00	05/28/82	-23.15	0.85	340.00	05/24/82	900.00	05/12/82	-1608.00
1981	04/27/81	-7.57	05/28/81	-2.65	4.92	1968.00	05/15/81	4700.00		

Percentage Correct	93									
Average Profit on Winning Trades					3.22	1288.00				
Average Loss on Trades					-5.15	-2060.00				
Average Net Profit Per Trade					2.66	1064.80				

Protective Stop	(1384)
Winners	14
Losers	1
Total trades	15

HYPOTHETICAL OR SIMULATED PERFORMANCE RESULTS HAVE CERTAIN INHERENT LIMITATIONS. UNLIKE AN ACTUAL PERFORMANCE RECORD, SIMULATED RESULTS DO NOT REPRESENT ACTUAL TRADING. ALSO, SINCE THE TRADES HAVE NOT ACTUALLY BEEN EXECUTED, THE RESULTS MAY HAVE UNDER-OR OVER-COMPENSATED FOR THE IMPACT, IF ANY, OF CERTAIN MARKET FACTORS, SUCH AS LACK OF LIQUIDITY. SIMULATED TRADING PROGRAMS IN GENERAL ARE ALSO SUBJECT TO THE FACT THAT THEY ARE DESIGNED WITH THE BENEFIT OF HINDSIGHT. NO REPRESENTATION IS BEING MADE THAT ANY ACCOUNT WILL OR IS LIKELY TO ACHIEVE PROFITS OR LOSSES SIMILAR TO THOSE SHOWN. SIMULATED RESULTS DO NOT NECESSARILY IMPLY FUTURE PROFITS. THE RISK OF LOSS IN TRADING COMMODITY CONTRACTS CAN BE SUBSTANTIAL. YOU SHOULD THEREFORE, CAREFULLY CONSIDER WHETHER SUCH TRADING IS SUITABLE FOR YOU IN LIGHT OF YOUR FINANCIAL CONDITION. RESULTS NOT ADJUSTED FOR COMMISSION AND SLIPPAGE.

May Spreads

Moore Research Center, Inc. — Futures Trade	Entry Date	Exit Date	Win Pct	Win Years	Loss Years	Total Years	Average Profit	Avg Pft Per Day
Buy Sep Canadian Dollar(IMM)- CDU[6] Sell Sep Swiss Franc(IMM)- SFU[6]	5/8	6/8	87	13	2	15	1135	36.60
Buy Jun Live Hogs(CME)- LHM[6] Sell Jun Live Cattle(CME)- LCM[6]	5/9	5/20	87	13	2	15	738	67.10
Buy Jul Corn(CBOT)- CN[6] Sell Jul Wheat(CBOT)- WN[6]	5/11	6/18	87	13	2	15	593	15.59
Buy Sep 30-Year T-Bonds(CBOT)- USU[6] Sell Sep 5-Year T-Notes(CBOT)- FVU[6]	5/14	5/31	89	8	1	9	840	49.41
Buy Jul Live Hogs(CME)- LHN[6] Sell Jul Pork Bellies(CME)- PBN[6]	5/16	7/4	93	14	1	15	1699	34.68
Buy Aug Soybean Meal(CBOT)- SMQ[6] Sell Aug Soybeans(CBOT)- SQ[6]	5/17	6/13	87	13	2	15	531	19.66
Buy Jun Japanese Yen(IMM)- JYM[6] Sell Jun British Pound(IMM)- BPM[6]	5/17	6/4	80	12	3	15	1521	84.51
Buy Aug Feeder Cattle(CME)- FCQ[6] Sell Oct Live Cattle(CME)- LCV[6]	5/20	8/19	93	14	1	15	1452	15.96
Buy Aug Gold(CMX)- GCQ[6] Sell Sep Silver(CMX)- SIU[6]	5/22	6/27	87	13	2	15	1724	47.89
Buy Oct Live Cattle(CME)- LCV[6] Sell Oct Live Hogs(CME)- LHV[6]	5/24	7/13	87	13	2	15	947	18.94

Buy Dec Soybean Meal(CBOT)- SMZ[6] **Sell Dec Soybean Oil(CBOT)- BOZ[6]**	5/27	6/16	80	12	3	15	562	28.08
Buy Aug Heating Oil(NYM)- HOQ[6] **Sell Aug Unleaded Gas(NYM)- HUQ[6]**	5/27	6/29	90	9	1	10	710	21.52
Buy Sep 30-Year T-Bonds(CBOT)- USU[6] **Sell Sep Municipal Bonds(CBOT)- MBU[6]**	5/31	7/2	91	10	1	11	1168	36.49

Note: One column in the above table equates each trade by its *impact* or daily return. Ave Pft Per Day quantifies the average historical profit (including losses) per day of trade maintenance, i.e., historical daily return.

Buy Sep 30-Yr T-Bonds(CBOT) / Sell Sep 5-Yr T-Notes(CBOT)

Moore Research Center, Inc.

Enter on approximately 05/14 - Exit on approximately 05/31

CONT YEAR	ENTRY DATE	ENTRY PRICE	EXIT DATE	EXIT PRICE	PROFIT	PROFIT AMOUNT	BEST EQUITY DATE	BEST EQUITY AMOUNT	WORST EQUITY DATE	WORST EQUITY AMOUNT
1995	05/15/95	3.60	05/31/95	5.46	1.86	1859.38	05/31/95	1859.38		
1994	05/16/94	-0.87	05/31/94	-1.31	-0.44	-437.50	05/17/94	812.50	05/23/94	-453.13
1993	05/14/93	-1.06	05/28/93	-0.48	0.58	578.13	05/27/93	1218.75	05/18/93	-390.63
1992	05/14/92	-4.84	05/29/92	-4.67	0.17	171.88	05/22/92	546.88	05/26/92	-203.13
1991	05/15/91	-6.14	05/31/91	-5.42	0.72	718.75	05/21/91	890.63		
1990	05/15/90	-5.25	06/01/90	-4.15	1.09	1093.75	06/01/90	1093.75	05/25/90	-359.38
1989	05/15/89	-6.09	06/01/89	-4.65	1.44	1437.50	05/26/89	1609.38		
1988	05/20/88	-11.90	05/31/88	-11.25	0.66	656.25	05/31/88	656.25		
1987	05/15/87	-9.34	06/01/87	-7.85	1.48	1484.38	05/26/87	2000.00	05/20/87	-562.50

Percentage Correct	89			Protective Stop			(1092)
Average Profit on Winning Trades		1.00	1000.00	Winners			8
Average Loss on Trades		-0.44	-437.50	Losers			1
Average Net Profit Per Trade		0.84	840.28	Total trades			9

HYPOTHETICAL OR SIMULATED PERFORMANCE RESULTS HAVE CERTAIN INHERENT LIMITATIONS. UNLIKE AN ACTUAL PERFORMANCE RECORD, SIMULATED RESULTS DO NOT REPRESENT ACTUAL TRADING. ALSO, SINCE THE TRADES HAVE NOT ACTUALLY BEEN EXECUTED THE RESULTS MAY HAVE UNDER-OR OVER-COMPENSATED FOR THE IMPACT, IF ANY, OF CERTAIN MARKET FACTORS, SUCH AS LACK OF LIQUIDITY. SIMULATED TRADING PROGRAMS IN GENERAL ARE ALSO SUBJECT TO THE FACT THAT THEY ARE DESIGNED WITH THE BENEFIT OF HINDSIGHT. NO REPRESENTATION IS BEING MADE THAT ANY ACCOUNT WILL OR IS LIKELY TO ACHIEVE PROFITS OR LOSSES SIMILAR TO THOSE SHOWN. SIMULATED RESULTS DO NOT NECESSARILY IMPLY FUTURE PROFITS. THE RISK OF LOSS IN TRADING COMMODITY CONTRACTS CAN BE SUBSTANTIAL. YOU SHOULD THEREFORE, CAREFULLY CONSIDER WHETHER SUCH TRADING IS SUITABLE FOR YOU IN LIGHT OF YOUR FINANCIAL CONDITION. RESULTS NOT ADJUSTED FOR COMMISSION AND SLIPPAGE.

June Spreads

Moore Research Center, Inc.

Futures Trade	Entry Date	Exit Date	Win Pct	Win Years	Loss Years	Total Years	Average Profit	Avg Pft Per Day
Buy Sep Corn(CBOT)- CU[6] / Sell Sep Wheat(CBOT)- WU[6]	6/5	6/20	93	14	1	15	524	34.94
Buy Dec Cotton(CTN)- CTZ[6] / Sell Oct Cotton(CTN)- CTV[6]	6/6	7/27	80	12	3	15	638	12.51
Buy Sep 30-Year T-Bonds(CBOT)- USU[6] / Sell Sep Municipal Bonds(CBOT)- MBU[6]	6/7	7/2	82	9	2	11	861	34.43
Buy Aug Live Hogs(CME)- LHQ[6] / Sell Aug Pork Bellies(CME)- PBQ[6]	6/9	7/13	87	13	2	15	1925	56.61
Buy Aug Live Hogs(CME)- LHQ[6] / Sell Oct Live Hogs(CME)- LHV[6]	6/9	7/25	87	13	2	15	490	10.66
Buy Sep 30-Year T-Bonds(CBOT)- USU[6] / Sell Sep 10-Year T-Notes(CBOT)- TYU[6]	6/10	7/3	86	12	2	14	478	20.77
Buy Sep Heating Oil(NYM)- HOU[6] / Sell Sep Unleaded Gas(NYM)- HUU[6]	6/18	7/26	91	10	1	11	564	14.84
Buy Oct Live Cattle(CME)- LCV[7] / Sell Feb Live Cattle(CME)- LCG[7]	6/22	8/7	93	14	1	15	611	13.28
Buy Dec Wheat(CBOT)- WZ[6] / Sell Nov Soybeans(CBOT)- SX[6]	6/23	7/27	87	13	2	15	1447	42.55
Buy Sep Soybean Meal(CBOT)- SMU[6] / Sell Sep Soybeans(CBOT)- SU[6]	6/23	8/12	93	14	1	15	1225	24.50

Buy Aug Feeder Cattle(CME)- FCQ[6] Sell Dec Live Cattle(CME)- LCZ[6]	6/23	8/20	93	14	1	15	1434	24.73
Buy Mar Wheat(CBOT)- WH[7] Sell Mar Corn(CBOT)- CH[7]	6/23	9/7	87	13	2	15	1064	14.00
Buy Sep Municipal Bonds(CBOT)- MBU[6] Sell Sep 30-Year T-Bonds(CBOT)- USU[6]	6/28	7/22	82	9	2	11	744	31.01
Buy Sep British Pound(IMM)- BPU[6] Sell Sep Japanese Yen(IMM)- JYU[6]	6/28	7/25	80	12	3	15	1116	41.33
Buy Sep 10-Year T-Notes(CBOT)- TYU[6] Sell Sep 30-Year T-Bonds(CBOT)- USU[6]	6/29	7/21	86	12	2	14	433	19.68

Note: One column in the above table equates each trade by its *impact* or daily return. <u>Ave Pft Per Day</u> quantifies the average historical profit (including losses) per day of trade maintenance, i.e., historical daily return.

Buy Dec Cotton(CTN) / Sell Oct Cotton(CTN)

Moore Research Center, Inc.

Enter on approximately 06/06 - Exit on approximately 07/27

CONT YEAR	ENTRY DATE	ENTRY PRICE	EXIT DATE	EXIT PRICE	PROFIT	PROFIT AMOUNT	BEST EQUITY DATE	BEST EQUITY AMOUNT	WORST EQUITY DATE	WORST EQUITY AMOUNT
1995	06/06/95	-6.25	07/27/95	-2.85	3.40	1700.00	07/20/95	2355.00	06/26/95	-750.00
1994	06/06/94	-1.60	07/27/94	-0.31	1.30	650.00	06/29/94	1025.00		
1993	06/07/93	-0.32	07/27/93	1.22	1.55	775.00	07/20/93	910.00	06/21/93	-145.00
1992	06/08/92	-0.34	07/27/92	-1.32	-0.99	-495.00	06/16/92	270.00	07/07/92	-635.00
1991	06/06/91	-4.90	07/26/91	0.22	5.13	2565.00	07/26/91	2565.00	06/07/91	-160.00
1990	06/06/90	-5.04	07/27/90	-3.97	1.07	535.00	06/18/90	1040.00	07/05/90	-35.00
1989	06/06/89	-0.32	07/27/89	0.95	1.28	640.00	07/27/89	640.00	06/07/89	-25.00
1988	06/06/88	-1.21	07/27/88	-1.18	0.02	10.00	06/21/88	270.00	07/20/88	-225.00
1987	06/08/87	-0.64	07/27/87	-1.69	-1.06	-530.00			06/17/87	-630.00
1986	06/06/86	0.39	07/25/86	0.90	0.50	250.00	07/25/86	250.00	07/07/86	-185.00
1985	06/06/85	0.78	07/26/85	0.03	-0.76	-380.00			07/23/85	-520.00
1984	06/06/84	-3.29	07/27/84	1.06	4.36	2180.00	07/27/84	2180.00		
1983	06/06/83	0.81	07/27/83	0.96	0.15	75.00	07/08/83	335.00	06/24/83	-70.00
1982	06/07/82	1.28	07/27/82	2.32	1.03	515.00	07/26/82	550.00	06/16/82	-140.00
1981	06/08/81	-1.49	07/27/81	0.67	2.16	1080.00	07/23/81	1085.00	06/25/81	-455.00
Percentage Correct	80									
Average Profit on Winning Trades					1.83	914.58				
Average Loss on Trades					-0.94	-468.33				
Average Net Profit Per Trade					1.28	638.00				

Protective Stop	(829)
Winners	12
Losers	3
Total trades	15

July Spreads

Moore Research Center, Inc.

Futures Trade	Entry Date	Exit Date	Win Pct	Win Years	Loss Years	Total Years	Average Profit	Avg Pft Per Day
Buy Aug Feeder Cattle(CME)- FCQ[6] / Sell Dec Live Cattle(CME)- LCZ[6]	7/1	8/6	87	13	2	15	843	23.41
Buy Sep Soybean Meal(CBOT)- SMU[6] / Sell Sep Soybeans(CBOT)- SU[6]	7/1	8/12	93	14	1	15	1025	24.39
Buy Sep Swiss Franc(IMM)- SFU[6] / Sell Sep Japanese Yen(IMM)- JYU[6]	7/4	7/28	80	12	3	15	1007	41.94
Buy 10M Sep Soybeans(CBOT)- SU[6] / Sell 25M Sep Corn(CBOT)- CU[6]	7/5	8/3	100	15	0	15	2118	73.05
Buy Dec 10-Year T-Notes(CBOT)- TYZ[6] / Sell Dec Municipal Bonds(CBOT)- MBZ[6]	7/6	9/27	90	9	1	10	709	8.55
Buy Dec Wheat(CBOT)- WZ[6] / Sell Nov Soybeans(CBOT)- SX[6]	7/7	8/8	87	13	2	15	1326	41.43
Buy Sep Heating Oil(NYM)- HOU[6] / Sell Sep Unleaded Gas(NYM)- HUU[6]	7/8	7/20	82	9	2	11	481	40.12
Buy Mar Wheat(CBOT)- WH[7] / Sell Jul Wheat(CBOT)- WN[7]	7/9	10/14	87	13	2	15	444	4.58
Buy Sep Wheat(KCBT)- KWU[6] / Sell Sep Corn(CBOT)- CU[6]	7/10	8/26	87	13	2	15	908	19.31
Buy Dec Coffee "C"(CSCE)- KCZ[6] / Sell Sep Coffee "C"(CSCE)- KCU[6]	7/12	8/21	80	12	3	15	1601	40.02

Trade								
Buy Jan Heating Oil(NYM)- HOF[7] Sell Mar Heating Oil(NYM)- HOH[7]	7/13	9/24	93	14	1	15	416	5.70
Buy Oct Unleaded Gas(NYM)- HUV[6] Sell Jan Unleaded Gas(NYM)- HUF[7]	7/19	8/21	91	10	1	11	606	18.36
Buy Oct Unleaded Gas(NYM)- HUV[6] Sell Oct Heating Oil(NYM)- HOV[6]	7/20	8/21	82	9	2	11	428	13.39
Buy Dec Crude Oil(NYM)- CLZ[6] Sell Apr Crude Oil(NYM)- CLJ[7]	7/21	9/29	92	11	1	12	627	8.96
Buy Oct Live Cattle(CME)- LCV[6] Sell Oct Live Hogs(CME)- LHV[6]	7/22	8/9	80	12	3	15	605	33.59

Note: One column in the above table equates each trade by its *impact* or daily return. <u>Ave Pft Per Day</u> quantifies the average historical profit (including losses) per day of trade maintenance, i.e., historical daily return.

Buy Dec Crude Oil(NYM) / Sell Apr Crude Oil(NYM)

Moore Research Center, Inc.

Enter on approximately 07/21 - Exit on approximately 09/29

CONT YEAR	ENTRY DATE	ENTRY PRICE	EXIT DATE	EXIT PRICE	PROFIT	PROFIT AMOUNT	BEST EQUITY DATE	BEST EQUITY AMOUNT	WORST EQUITY DATE	WORST EQUITY AMOUNT
1995	07/21/95	-0.16	09/29/95	0.28	0.44	440.00	09/15/95	630.00	07/24/95	-10.00
1994	07/21/94	0.22	09/29/94	-0.17	-0.40	-400.00	08/01/94	290.00	09/15/94	-630.00
1993	07/21/93	-0.40	09/29/93	-0.30	0.10	100.00	09/29/93	100.00	09/15/93	-480.00
1992	07/21/92	0.41	09/29/92	0.42	0.00	0.00	07/28/92	180.00	08/20/92	-90.00
1991	07/22/91	0.57	09/27/91	0.82	0.25	250.00	08/19/91	310.00	09/09/91	-170.00
1990	07/23/90	-0.07	09/28/90	5.31	5.38	5380.00	09/26/90	5540.00		
1989	07/21/89	0.27	09/29/89	0.62	0.34	340.00	09/29/89	340.00	07/24/89	-230.00
1988	07/21/88	-0.19	09/29/88	0.08	0.28	280.00	09/28/88	300.00	09/07/88	-90.00
1987	07/21/87	0.15	09/29/87	0.25	0.10	100.00	08/04/87	310.00	08/20/87	-260.00
1986	07/21/86	0.00	09/29/86	0.21	0.22	220.00	09/02/86	570.00	07/31/86	-320.00
1985	07/22/85	0.98	09/27/85	1.63	0.64	640.00	09/26/85	720.00	07/29/85	-270.00
1984	07/23/84	0.17	09/28/84	0.35	0.17	170.00	07/27/84	430.00	08/08/84	-60.00
Percentage Correct	92									(815)
Average Profit on Winning Trades					0.72	720.00	Protective Stop		Winners	11
Average Loss on Trades					-0.40	-400.00			Losers	1
Average Net Profit Per Trade					0.63	626.67			Total trades	12

August Spreads

Futures Trade	Entry Date	Exit Date	Win Pct	Win Years	Loss Years	Total Years	Average Profit	Avg Pft Per Day
Buy Oct Unleaded Gas(NYM)- HUV[6] Sell Oct Crude Oil(NYM)- CLV[6]	8/1	8/21	82	9	2	11	741	37.04
Buy Jan Heating Oil(NYM)- HOF[7] Sell Apr Heating Oil(NYM)- HOJ[7]	8/3	9/26	93	14	1	15	534	9.89
Buy Mar Wheat(CBOT)- WH[7] Sell Mar Corn(CBOT)- CH[7]	8/5	8/30	87	13	2	15	418	16.70
Buy Jan Heating Oil(NYM)- HOF[7] Sell Jan Unleaded Gas(NYM)- HUF[7]	8/8	9/10	91	10	1	11	502	15.23
Buy Dec Wheat(KCBT)- KWZ[6] Sell Jul Wheat(KCBT)- KWN[7]	8/9	11/20	87	13	2	15	734	7.13
Buy Mar Soybeans(CBOT)- SH[7] Sell 10M Mar Corn(CBOT)- CH[7]	8/13	9/8	93	14	1	15	617	23.72
Buy Dec Swiss Franc(IMM)- SFZ[6] Sell Dec Canadian Dollar(IMM)- CDZ[6]	8/16	10/17	87	13	2	15	2101	33.89
Buy Dec Live Cattle(CME)- LCZ[6] Sell Jun Live Cattle(CME)- LCM[7]	8/20	10/12	93	14	1	15	628	11.85
Buy Dec Live Cattle(CME)- LCZ[6] Sell Dec Live Hogs(CME)- LHZ[6]	8/20	11/9	80	12	3	15	899	11.10
Buy Nov Crude Oil(NYM)- CLX[6] Sell Nov Unleaded Gas(NYM)- HUX[6]	8/22	9/22	82	9	2	11	540	17.43

Moore Research Center, Inc.

Buy Dec 10-Year T-Notes(CBOT)- TYZ[6] Sell Dec Municipal Bonds(CBOT)- MBZ[6]	8/26	9/27	100	10	0	10	656	20.51
Buy Jan Soybean Meal(CBOT)- SMF[7] Sell Jan Soybeans(CBOT)- SF[7]	8/26	10/6	93	14	1	15	771	18.79
Buy Dec Silver(CMX)- SIZ[6] Sell Dec Gold(CMX)- GCZ[6]	8/30	9/10	80	12	3	15	809	73.58
Buy Dec Wheat(CBOT)- WZ[6] Sell Nov Soybeans(CBOT)- SX[6]	8/30	10/26	87	13	2	15	1500	26.32
Buy Dec Crude Oil(NYM)- CLZ[6] Sell Jun Crude Oil(NYM)- CLM[7]	8/31	9/30	92	11	1	12	572	19.06

Note: One column in the above table equates each trade by its *impact* or daily return. **Ave Pft Per Day** quantifies the average historical profit (including losses) per day of trade maintenance, i.e., historical daily return.

Buy Mar Wheat(CBOT) / Sell Mar Corn(CBOT)

Moore Research Center, Inc.

Enter on approximately 08/05 - Exit on approximately 08/30

CONT YEAR	ENTRY DATE	ENTRY PRICE	EXIT DATE	EXIT PRICE	PROFIT	PROFIT AMOUNT	BEST EQUITY DATE	BEST EQUITY AMOUNT	WORST EQUITY DATE	WORST EQUITY AMOUNT
1996	08/07/95	148.50	08/30/95	151.25	2.75	137.50	08/11/95	787.50	08/17/95	-12.50
1995	08/05/94	126.75	08/30/94	152.25	25.50	1275.00	08/30/94	1275.00	08/09/94	-250.00
1994	08/05/93	64.75	08/30/93	67.00	2.25	112.50	08/17/93	437.50	08/12/93	-75.00
1993	08/05/92	96.25	08/28/92	108.75	12.50	625.00	08/25/92	712.50	08/17/92	-375.00
1992	08/05/91	45.00	08/30/91	62.25	17.25	862.50	08/30/91	862.50		
1991	08/06/90	49.75	08/30/90	51.75	2.00	100.00	08/09/90	512.50	08/07/90	-62.50
1990	08/07/89	176.25	08/30/89	161.00	-15.25	-762.50	08/09/89	250.00	08/30/89	-762.50
1989	08/05/88	77.50	08/30/88	123.00	45.50	2275.00	08/30/88	2275.00		
1988	08/05/87	105.50	08/28/87	116.75	11.25	562.50	08/25/87	675.00		
1987	08/05/86	80.00	08/29/86	81.50	1.50	75.00	08/29/86	75.00	08/21/86	-362.50
1986	08/05/85	63.75	08/30/85	65.75	2.00	100.00	08/15/85	812.50	08/29/85	-37.50
1985	08/06/84	89.25	08/30/84	69.25	-20.00	-1000.00	08/10/84	162.50	08/27/84	-1137.50
1984	08/05/83	47.50	08/30/83	56.25	8.75	437.50	08/22/83	612.50	08/23/83	-137.50
1983	08/05/82	120.75	08/30/82	137.00	16.25	812.50	08/19/82	937.50	08/10/82	-187.50
1982	08/05/81	113.00	08/28/81	126.00	13.00	650.00	08/14/81	1125.00		

Percentage Correct	87						Protective Stop	(543)
Average Profit on Winning Trades					12.35	617.31	Winners	13
Average Loss on Trades					-17.63	-881.25	Losers	2
Average Net Profit Per Trade					8.35	417.50	Total trades	15

September Spreads

Moore Research Center, Inc. Futures Trade	Entry Date	Exit Date	Win Pct	Win Years	Loss Years	Total Years	Average Profit	Avg Pft Per Day
Buy Nov Crude Oil(NYM)- CLX[6] Sell Mar Crude Oil(NYM)- CLH[7]	9/4	10/10	92	12	1	13	491	13.63
Buy Dec Swiss Franc(IMM)- SFZ[6] Sell Dec Deutsche Mark(IMM)- DMZ[6]	9/7	10/2	80	12	3	15	616	24.63
Buy Dec Wheat(KCBT)- KWZ[6] Sell Jul Wheat(KCBT)- KWN[7]	9/10	11/21	87	13	2	15	488	6.78
Buy 10M Dec Corn(CBOT)- CZ[6] Sell Nov Soybeans(CBOT)- SX[6]	9/11	10/3	100	15	0	15	960	43.64
Buy Dec 30-Year T-Bonds(CBOT)- USZ[6] Sell Dec Municipal Bonds(CBOT)- MBZ[6]	9/11	10/6	90	9	1	10	600	24.00
Buy Nov Heating Oil(NYM)- HOX[6] Sell Nov Unleaded Gas(NYM)- HUX[6]	9/16	10/5	82	9	2	11	733	38.58
Buy 10M Mar Wheat(KCBT)- KWH[7] Sell Mar Soybeans(CBOT)- SH[7]	9/17	10/5	100	15	0	15	1193	66.30
Buy Dec Heating Oil(NYM)- HOZ[6] Sell May Heating Oil(NYM)- HOK[7]	9/17	10/20	87	13	2	15	587	17.78
Buy Mar Wheat(CBOT)- WH[7] Sell Mar Corn(CBOT)- CH[7]	9/18	10/24	87	13	2	15	440	12.22
Buy Dec Live Cattle(CME)- LCZ[6] Sell Jun Live Cattle(CME)- LCM[7]	9/19	10/17	93	14	1	15	413	14.74

Trade								
Buy Dec Live Cattle(CME)- LCZ[6] Sell Jan Feeder Cattle(CME)- FCF[7]	9/19	11/8	93	14	1	15	588	11.75
Buy Dec Live Cattle(CME)- LCZ[6] Sell Dec Live Hogs(CME)- LHZ[6]	9/19	11/25	87	13	2	15	689	10.28
Buy Dec Soybean Meal(CBOT)- SMZ[6] Sell Nov Soybeans(CBOT)- SX[6]	9/21	10/2	93	14	1	15	421	38.24
Buy Dec 30-Year T-Bonds(CBOT)- USZ[6] Sell Dec 10-Year T-Notes(CBOT)- TYZ[6]	9/22	10/31	86	12	2	14	752	19.29
Buy Mar Soybean Meal(CBOT)- SMH[7] Sell Mar Soybean Oil(CBOT)- BOH[7]	9/27	11/4	80	12	3	15	555	14.59

Note: One column in the above table equates each trade by its *impact* or daily return. <u>Ave Pft Per Day</u> quantifies the average historical profit (including losses) per day of trade maintenance, i.e., historical daily return.

Moore Research Center, Inc. — Buy Dec Heating Oil #2(NYM) / Sell May Heating Oil #2(NYM)

Enter on approximately 09/17 - Exit on approximately 10/20

CONT YEAR	ENTRY DATE	ENTRY PRICE	EXIT DATE	EXIT PRICE	PROFIT	PROFIT AMOUNT	BEST EQUITY DATE	BEST EQUITY AMOUNT	WORST EQUITY DATE	WORST EQUITY AMOUNT
1995	09/18/95	4.50	10/20/95	2.33	-2.16	-907.20			10/19/95	-991.20
1994	09/19/94	0.21	10/20/94	0.95	0.73	306.60	10/20/94	306.60	10/13/94	-533.40
1993	09/17/93	1.29	10/20/93	1.80	0.50	210.00	09/30/93	1029.00		
1992	09/17/92	6.30	10/20/92	6.41	0.11	46.20	10/09/92	550.20	09/21/92	-75.60
1991	09/17/91	7.21	10/18/91	9.91	2.70	1134.00	10/17/91	1209.60		
1990	09/17/90	12.42	10/19/90	18.22	5.81	2440.20	10/12/90	3675.00		
1989	09/18/89	6.90	10/20/89	8.12	1.22	512.40	10/12/89	743.40	09/19/89	-25.20
1988	09/19/88	3.35	10/20/88	5.12	1.78	747.60	10/19/88	898.80	09/30/88	-310.80
1987	09/17/87	3.28	10/20/87	5.22	1.94	814.80	10/09/87	1066.80	09/21/87	-58.80
1986	09/17/86	4.00	10/20/86	1.84	-2.16	-907.20	09/19/86	163.80	10/10/86	-1423.80
1985	09/17/85	9.46	10/18/85	10.50	1.04	436.80	10/07/85	735.00	09/23/85	-33.60
1984	09/17/84	4.75	10/19/84	5.48	0.73	306.60	09/26/84	831.60	09/24/84	-420.00
1983	09/19/83	4.62	10/20/83	4.85	0.22	92.40	10/10/83	588.00	09/28/83	-84.00
1982	09/17/82	5.21	10/20/82	10.82	5.61	2356.20	10/20/82	2356.20	09/20/82	-222.60
1981	09/17/81	-4.04	10/20/81	-1.15	2.89	1213.80	10/15/81	1268.40	09/22/81	-16.80

Percentage Correct	87						Protective Stop	(763)		
Average Profit on Winning Trades					1.94	816.74	Winners	13		
Average Loss on Trades					-2.16	-907.20	Losers	2		
Average Net Profit Per Trade					1.40	586.88	Total trades	15		

Moore Research Center, Inc.

October Spreads

Futures Trade	Entry Date	Exit Date	Win Pct	Win Years	Loss Years	Total Years	Average Profit	Avg Pft Per Day
Buy Dec Japanese Yen(IMM)- JYZ[6] / Sell Dec British Pound(IMM)- BPZ[6]	10/6	10/16	87	13	2	15	995	99.50
Buy Dec 30-Year T-Bonds(CBOT)- USZ[6] / Sell Dec 10-Year T-Notes(CBOT)- TYZ[6]	10/6	10/31	86	12	2	14	538	21.52
Buy Dec Unleaded Gas(NYM)- HUZ[6] / Sell Dec Heating Oil(NYM)- HOZ[6]	10/6	10/31	91	10	1	11	924	36.94
Buy Dec Live Cattle(CME)- LCZ[6] / Sell Jun Live Cattle(CME)- LCM[7]	10/6	11/18	87	13	2	15	526	12.22
Buy Feb Pork Bellies(CME)- PBG[7] / Sell Dec Live Hogs(CME)- LHZ[6]	10/9	10/20	87	13	2	15	719	65.33
Buy May Pork Bellies(CME)- PBK[7] / Sell Apr Lean Hogs(CME)- LHJ[7]	10/9	10/22	87	13	2	15	780	59.98
Buy Dec 30-Year T-Bonds(CBOT)- USZ[6] / Sell Dec Municipal Bonds(CBOT)- MBZ[6]	10/17	10/31	90	9	1	10	563	40.18
Buy Dec British Pound(IMM)- BPZ[6] / Sell Dec Japanese Yen(IMM)- JYZ[6]	10/17	11/5	80	12	3	15	1360	71.60
Buy Mar Unleaded Gas(NYM)- HUH[7] / Sell Jan Unleaded Gas(NYM)- HUF[7]	10/20	12/10	91	10	1	11	505	9.90
Buy Apr Lean Hogs(CME)- LHJ[7] / Sell May Pork Bellies(CME)- PBK[7]	10/23	12/8	87	13	2	15	906	19.70

Buy May Orange Juice(CTN)- JOK[7] **Sell Jan Orange Juice(CTN)- JOF[7]**	10/26	1/2	93	14	1	15	425	6.44
Buy Mar Soybeans(CBOT)- SH[7] **Sell Mar Corn(CBOT)- CH[7]**	10/29	11/4	93	14	1	15	426	70.97
Buy Jun Lean Hogs(CME)- LHM[7] **Sell Feb Lean Hogs(CME)- LHG[7]**	10/31	1/10	93	14	1	15	562	7.91

Note: One column in the above table equates each trade by its *impact* or daily return. <u>Ave Pft Per Day</u> quantifies the average historical profit (including losses) per day of trade maintenance, i.e., historical daily return.

Moore Research Center, Inc. — Buy May 97 Orange Juice(CTN) / Sell Jan 97 Orange Juice(CTN)

Enter on approximately 10/26 - Exit on approximately 01/02 - Caution: This Trade Enters Deliverable Period

CONT YEAR	ENTRY DATE	ENTRY PRICE	EXIT DATE	EXIT PRICE	PROFIT	PROFIT AMOUNT	BEST EQUITY DATE	BEST EQUITY AMOUNT	WORST EQUITY DATE	WORST EQUITY AMOUNT
1996	10/26/95	4.10	01/02/96	5.75	1.65	247.50	12/12/95	637.50	11/01/95	-135.00
1995	10/26/94	6.29	12/30/94	7.45	1.15	172.50	11/21/94	765.00	11/17/94	-52.50
1994	10/26/93	3.84	12/30/93	6.00	2.15	322.50	12/22/93	375.00	11/12/93	-97.50
1993	10/26/92	2.70	12/31/92	6.50	3.80	570.00	12/23/92	615.00	11/24/92	-315.00
1992	10/28/91	-0.44	01/02/92	1.59	2.05	307.50	11/19/91	780.00		
1991	10/26/90	0.50	01/02/91	8.65	8.15	1222.50	01/02/91	1222.50	12/20/90	-427.50
1990	10/26/89	0.70	01/02/90	-3.25	-3.95	-592.50	11/06/89	82.50	12/26/89	-1920.00
1989	10/26/88	-4.44	12/30/88	-1.04	3.40	510.00	12/21/88	742.50	11/02/88	-22.50
1988	10/26/87	0.30	12/31/87	3.75	3.45	517.50	12/30/87	577.50	11/10/87	-525.00
1987	10/27/86	0.09	12/31/86	3.09	3.00	450.00	12/29/86	690.00	11/03/86	-52.50
1986	10/28/85	-0.70	01/02/86	4.50	5.20	780.00	12/27/85	870.00	10/30/85	-22.50
1985	10/26/84	0.75	01/02/85	3.90	3.15	472.50	12/28/84	480.00	11/02/84	-127.50
1984	10/26/83	-3.20	12/30/83	5.09	8.30	1245.00	12/30/83	1245.00	10/28/83	-22.50
1983	10/26/82	2.59	12/30/82	2.94	0.35	52.50	12/30/82	52.50	12/10/82	-120.00
1982	10/26/81	4.75	12/31/81	5.34	0.60	90.00	11/05/81	135.00	11/23/81	-427.50

Percentage Correct	93						Protective Stop	(552)		
Average Profit on Winning Trades					3.31	497.14	Winners	14		
Average Loss on Trades					-3.95	-592.50	Losers	1		
Average Net Profit Per Trade					2.83	424.50	Total trades	15		

November Spreads

Moore Research Center, Inc.

Futures Trade	Entry Date	Exit Date	Win Pct	Win Years	Loss Years	Total Years	Average Profit	Avg Pft Per Day
Buy Mar Municipal Bonds(CBOT)- MBH[7] / Sell Mar 10-Year T-Notes(CBOT)- TYH[7]*	11/1	1/7	91	10	1	11	1250	18.66
Buy May Orange Juice(CTN)- JOK[7] / Sell Jan Orange Juice(CTN)- JOF[7]*	11/4	1/4	100	15	0	15	397	6.51
Buy Mar Deutsche Mark(IMM)- DMH[7] / Sell Mar Swiss Franc(IMM)- SFH[7]	11/9	2/10	87	13	2	15	873	9.39
Buy Jun Lean Hogs(CME)- LEM[7] / Sell Feb Lean Hogs(CME)- LEG[7]	11/11	1/10	93	14	1	15	638	10.63
Buy Nov Soybeans(CBOT)- SX[7] / Sell Jul Soybeans(CBOT)- SN[7]	11/1	2/8	93	14	1	15	941	10.57
Buy Feb Unleaded Gas(NYM)- HUG[7] / Sell Jan Unleaded Gas(NYM)- HUF[7]	11/13	12/10	82	9	2	11	425	1.08
Buy 10M Mar Soybeans(CBOT)- SH[7] / Sell 25M Mar Corn(CBOT)- CH[7]	11/18	12/4	93	14	1	15	1170	3.07
Buy Feb Lean Hogs(CME)- LEG[7] / Sell Feb Pork Bellies(CME)- PBG[7]	11/21	12/3	93	14	1	15	558	1.48
Buy Mar Copper(CMX)- HGH[7] / Sell Jul Copper(CMX)- HGN[7]	11/21	12/31	87	13	2	15	478	1.18
Buy Apr Gold(CMX)- GCJ[7] / Sell 2 Apr Platinum(NYM)- PLJ[7]	11/22	12/29	87	13	2	15	1137	2.83

Buy Jul Wheat(CBOT)- WN[7] Sell Mar Wheat(CBOT)- WH[7]	11/24	2/13	93	14	1	15	458	5.65
Buy Mar 30-Year T-Bonds(CBOT)- USH[7] Sell Mar 10-Year T-Notes(CBOT)- TYH[7]	11/29	12/27	93	13	1	14	763	1.94
Buy Mar Soybean Oil(CBOT)- BOH[7] Sell Mar Soybean Meal(CBOT)- SMH[7]	11/30	12/21	80	12	3	15	445	1.15

Note: One column in the above table equates each trade by its *impact* or daily return. Ave Pft Per Day quantifies the average historical profit (including losses) per day of trade maintenance, i.e., historical daily return.

Note: These trade strategies have worked with historical consistency. No representation is being made that they will work this year or in the future. Please check current market fundamentals and technical conditions before considering these trades. This information is not a recommendation to buy or sell at this time, but merely a historical presentation of trade strategies. Past results are not necessarily indicative of future results. No representation is being made that an account will or is likely to achieve profits or incur losses similar to those shown.

Buy Mar Deutsche Mark(IMM) / Sell Mar Swiss Franc(IMM)

Enter on approximately 11/09 - Exit on approximately 02/10

CONT YEAR	ENTRY DATE	ENTRY PRICE	EXIT DATE	EXIT PRICE	PROFIT	PROFIT AMOUNT	BEST EQUITY DATE	BEST EQUITY AMOUNT	WORST EQUITY DATE	WORST EQUITY AMOUNT
1996	11/09/95	-17.80	02/09/96	-15.29	2.51	3137.50	02/02/96	3500.00	11/10/95	-137.50
1995	11/09/94	-12.87	02/10/95	-12.27	0.60	750.00	12/08/94	1575.00	01/10/95	-100.00
1994	11/09/93	-8.19	02/10/94	-10.65	-2.45	-3062.50	11/11/93	250.00	02/03/94	-4225.00
1993	11/09/92	-7.64	02/10/93	-4.94	2.70	3375.00	02/08/93	3387.50	12/02/92	-1137.50
1992	11/11/91	-8.27	02/10/92	-7.71	0.56	700.00	02/04/92	787.50	12/06/91	-437.50
1991	11/09/90	-12.92	02/08/91	-11.78	1.14	1425.00	12/20/90	2675.00	01/14/91	-337.50
1990	11/09/89	-7.64	02/09/90	-7.04	0.60	750.00	01/02/90	3687.50	01/25/90	-200.00
1989	11/09/88	-11.11	02/10/89	-9.48	1.63	2037.50	01/16/89	2350.00	11/29/88	-512.50
1988	11/09/87	-13.37	02/10/88	-13.18	0.18	225.00	11/12/87	700.00	12/31/87	-2400.00
1987	11/10/86	-10.16	02/10/87	-10.15	0.01	12.50	12/16/86	1275.00	01/19/87	-800.00
1986	11/11/85	-8.53	02/10/86	-8.13	0.41	512.50	01/17/86	1575.00	11/22/85	-375.00
1985	11/09/84	-7.53	02/08/85	-5.33	2.20	2750.00	02/08/85	2750.00	11/12/84	-137.50
1984	11/09/83	-9.14	02/10/84	-8.50	0.65	812.50	02/09/84	825.00	12/27/83	-637.50
1983	11/09/82	-7.05	02/10/83	-8.15	-1.11	-1387.50	11/11/82	487.50	01/13/83	-3287.50
1982	11/09/81	-11.42	02/10/82	-10.57	0.85	1062.50	12/09/81	1650.00	11/13/81	-1000.00

Percentage Correct	87						Protective Stop			(1135)
Average Profit on Winning Trades					1.08	1350.00	Winners			13
Average Loss on Trades					-1.78	-2225.00	Losers			2
Average Net Profit Per Trade					0.70	873.33	Total trades			15

Moore Research Center, Inc.

December Spreads

Futures Trade	Entry Date	Exit Date	Win Pct	Win Years	Loss Years	Total Years	Average Profit	Avg Pft Per Day
Buy Mar Heating Oil(NYM)- HOH[7] Sell Jun Heating Oil(NYM)- HOM[7]	12/7	12/27	93	14	1	15	429	21.46
Buy Nov Soybeans(CBOT)- SX[7] Sell Jul Soybeans(CBOT)- SN[7]	12/9	2/10	93	14	1	15	1043	16.55
Buy Jun Lean Hogs(CME)- LEM[7] Sell Feb Lean Hogs(CME)- LEG[7]	12/16	1/11	93	14	1	15	575	22.12
Buy Mar Eurodollars(IMM)- EDH[7] Sell Mar 3-Mth T-Bills(IMM)- TBH[7]	12/16	2/8	86	12	2	14	384	7.11
Buy Mar Municipal Bonds(CBOT)- MBH[7] Sell Mar 10-Year T-Notes(CBOT)- TYH[7]	12/18	1/3	91	10	1	11	642	40.13
Buy 25M Jul Corn(CBOT)- CN[7] Sell 10M Jul Soybeans(CBOT)- SN[7]	12/19	2/4	93	14	1	15	1958	41.67
Buy Apr Live Cattle(CME)- LCJ[7] Sell Aug Live Cattle(CME)- LCQ[7]	12/22	2/26	87	13	2	15	718	10.88
Buy Jul Wheat(CBOT)- WN[7] Sell Mar Wheat(CBOT)- WH[7]	12/23	2/13	87	13	2	15	498	9.57
Buy Jul Wheat(CBOT)- WN[7] Sell Jul Soybeans(CBOT)- SN[7]	12/24	2/22	93	14	1	15	962	16.03
Buy Mar Unleaded Gas(NYM)- HUH[7] Sell Mar Heating Oil(NYM)- HOH[7]	12/27	2/4	91	10	1	11	1266	32.47

Moore Research Center, Inc.

Buy Apr Live Cattle(CME)- LCJ[7] Sell Apr Lean Hogs(CME)- LEJ[7]	12/27	2/22	87	13	2	15	876	15.37
Buy Mar Deutsche Mark(IMM)- DMH[7] Sell Mar Swiss Franc(IMM)- SFH[7]	12/28	2/23	80	12	3	15	668	11.71
Buy Mar Canadian Dollar(IMM)- CDH[7] Sell Mar British Pound(IMM)- BPH[7]	12/29	2/12	80	12	3	15	1668	37.07
Buy 2 Apr Platinum(NYM)- PLJ[7] Sell Apr Gold(CMX)- GCJ[7]	12/30	2/15	100	15	0	15	1902	40.47
Buy Jun Lean Hogs(CME)- LEM[7] Sell Jul Pork Bellies(CME)- PBN[7]	12/30	3/1	93	14	1	15	1570	25.74

Note: One column in the above table equates each trade by its *impact* or daily return. Ave Pft Per Day quantifies the average historical profit (including losses) per day of trade maintenance, i.e., historical daily return.

Buy Jun Lean Hogs(CME) / Sell Feb Lean Hogs(CME)

Enter on approximately 12/16 - Exit on approximately 01/11

Moore Research Center, Inc.

CONT YEAR	ENTRY DATE	ENTRY PRICE	EXIT DATE	EXIT PRICE	PROFIT	PROFIT AMOUNT	BEST EQUITY DATE	BEST EQUITY AMOUNT	WORST EQUITY DATE	WORST EQUITY AMOUNT
1996	12/18/95	6.10	01/11/96	7.77	1.67	668.00	01/09/96	804.00		
1995	12/16/94	7.12	01/11/95	7.35	0.23	92.00	01/06/95	996.00	12/28/94	-296.00
1994	12/16/93	8.83	01/11/94	9.05	0.23	92.00	12/28/93	588.00	12/17/93	-56.00
1993	12/16/92	3.57	01/11/93	5.70	2.12	848.00	01/06/93	1028.00		
1992	12/16/91	4.58	01/10/92	6.01	1.42	568.00	01/09/92	608.00	12/20/91	-296.00
1991	12/17/90	1.35	01/11/91	4.65	3.31	1324.00	01/10/91	1420.00		
1990	12/18/89	-0.84	01/11/90	2.14	2.99	1196.00	01/10/90	1256.00	12/19/89	-160.00
1989	12/16/88	4.63	01/11/89	5.77	1.15	460.00	01/11/89	460.00	12/23/88	-572.00
1988	12/16/87	-0.33	01/11/88	2.10	2.44	976.00	01/11/88	976.00		
1987	12/16/86	-4.18	01/09/87	-2.60	1.59	636.00	01/02/87	892.00	12/17/86	-84.00
1986	12/16/85	-3.42	01/10/86	-1.21	2.20	880.00	01/02/86	1068.00		
1985	12/17/84	-1.60	01/11/85	2.59	4.20	1680.00	01/11/85	1680.00		
1984	12/16/83	5.40	01/11/84	1.65	-3.75	-1500.00			01/10/84	-1592.00
1983	12/16/82	-2.82	01/11/83	-2.78	0.04	16.00	12/22/82	496.00	01/06/83	-304.00
1982	12/16/81	1.42	01/11/82	3.14	1.73	692.00	12/29/81	828.00		

Percentage Correct	93						Protective Stop			(748)
Average Profit on Winning Trades					1.81	723.43	Winners			14
Average Loss on Trades					-3.75	-1500.00	Losers			1
Average Net Profit Per Trade					1.44	575.20	Total trades			15

Buy Mar 96 Value-Line(KCBT) / Sell Mar 96 S&P 500(CME)

Enter on approximately 12/19 - Exit on approximately 01/11

CONT YEAR	ENTRY DATE	ENTRY PRICE	EXIT DATE	EXIT PRICE	PROFIT	PROFIT AMOUNT	BEST EQUITY DATE	BEST EQUITY AMOUNT	WORST EQUITY DATE	WORST EQUITY AMOUNT
1996	12/19/95	-46.60	01/11/96	-44.84	1.75	875.00	12/21/95	3275.00	01/09/96	-1800.00
1995	12/19/94	-12.35	01/11/95	-9.05	3.30	1650.00	01/03/95	3450.00		
1994	12/20/93	-14.90	01/11/94	-14.55	0.35	175.00	01/05/94	2975.00	12/22/93	-1875.00
1993	12/21/92	-60.64	01/11/93	-45.54	15.10	7550.00	01/11/93	7550.00		
1992	12/19/91	-75.30	01/10/92	-72.84	2.45	1225.00	01/09/92	1625.00	12/30/91	-2725.00
1991	12/19/90	-89.75	01/11/91	-82.10	7.65	3825.00	01/09/91	4575.00	12/21/90	-700.00
1990	12/19/89	-61.00	01/11/90	-59.65	1.35	675.00	01/05/90	1100.00	01/02/90	-1175.00
1989	12/19/88	-36.00	01/11/89	-32.80	3.20	1600.00	01/05/89	2800.00		
1988	12/21/87	-48.40	01/11/88	-45.09	3.30	1650.00	01/08/88	1975.00	12/23/87	-775.00
1987	12/19/86	-19.69	01/09/87	-16.89	2.80	1400.00	01/08/87	1625.00	12/29/86	-425.00
1986	12/19/85	3.64	01/10/86	4.84	1.20	600.00	01/06/86	1725.00		
1985	12/19/84	12.29	01/11/85	15.84	3.55	1775.00	01/11/85	1775.00	12/20/84	-100.00
1984	12/19/83	29.80	01/11/84	33.60	3.80	1900.00	01/11/84	1900.00	12/29/83	-625.00
1983	12/20/82	17.00	01/11/83	23.00	6.00	3000.00	01/11/83	3000.00	12/27/82	-50.00
Percentage Correct	100									
Average Profit on Winning Trades					3.99	1992.86		Protective Stop		(2591)
Average Loss on Trades								Winners		14
								Losers		0
Average Net Profit Per Trade					3.99	1992.86		Total trades		14

Moore Research Center, Inc.

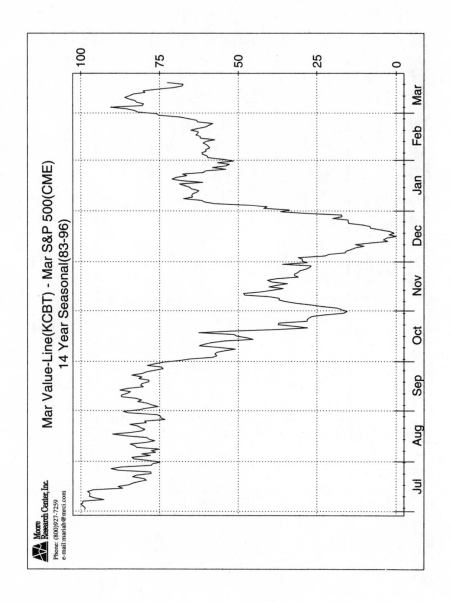

Mar Value-Line(KCBT) - Mar S&P 500(CME)
14 Year Seasonal(83-96)

Moore
Research Center, Inc.
Phone: (800)927-7259
e-mail:mariah@mrci.com

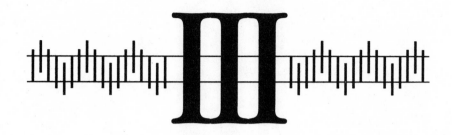
The Top Traders
and
Market Experts

CHAPTER 6

F. McCoy Coan

*"Coy" Coan was a longtime member
of the Chicago Board of Trade. He is presently a
consultant to agribusiness companies.*

Q: How did you first get interested in trading?

Coy: I've really been interested in trading all my life. I started trading cotton when I was 13 years old. I guess I just kind of got the bug from an early age. I've been doing it now for 46 years.

Q: You're not that old, are you?

Coy: Yes, I am!

Q: What were some of your early trading experiences like?

Coy: I'd like to tell you about one specific spread trade that I was in that really stands out. It was the July/November 1973 bean spread. I don't think there's any question that it was one of the most volatile grain trades of all. I'll never forget it! A large grain company went out of business because they were short the spread: short the July and long the November. I was the other way, I remember the spread was a huge mover. The spread moved from 20 cents premium July to $3.05 premium July, and I was involved with a big, big spread position. Can't help but remember that!

Beans made an all-time high of $12.90. It was a big bull market. It was that market in 1973 that got me turned on toward spreads. It made me realize that there was a tremendous profit potential in spreading and it was a way to have a market position and manage risk in a way that you don't get caught one way as you do in an outright long or short position.

Q: In what way?

Coy: In the sense that spreading offers a tremendous amount of options. Once the market declares a long-term direction, even if you were the wrong way initially, spreading offers you the opportunity to lift a leg or ratio or butterfly. In other words, it provides you with more ways to manage your money and the risk. There is another thing that I learned from 1973 that needs to be mentioned and that is that fundamentals are the dominant factor in trading. Of course the technical stuff is important but I believe it is the fundamentals that drive the spreads.

Q: Specifically, how did your trading experience in 1973 help you to formulate your current market approach?

Coy: It taught me to focus on the recurring nature of fundamental situations, in other words, to pay attention to particular situations where a certain sequence of events begin to materialize. I know when certain fundamental patterns arise there is a high degree of probability that the market and spread differential will move in an historic or cyclical manner that I can profit from.

Q: Your trading focuses primarily on the grain market. Is that correct?

Coy: I'd say 90 percent of my trading is involved in the grain complex: corn, beans, wheat meal, and bean oil.

Q: You mentioned the recurring nature of fundamental situations. Are you referring specifically to the seasonal patterns, that is, the cyclical nature of planting and harvesting and the demand and sales of grain exports?

Coy: Of course, all of those things have a bearing on the market. But in analysis they're just discrete pieces of a much larger puzzle. When it comes to corn or beans or wheat, I'm scrupulously watching the changing ratios of carry out and world crop size versus the previous year. I'm also factoring in government or cultural policy in the U.S. or Canada or the E.U. or Australia. There is a vast pool of information that you have to assimilate. Once you do, you can observe patterns beginning to develop, and I've found that what I do is formulate a spread position that allows me to exploit an emergency fundamental condition with a minimum risk and a maximum reward potential.

Q: So you try to anticipate what the market is going to do based on your assimilation of the fundamental data. Is that correct?

Coy: Right. We watch for a time frame in which we know market events begin to shape up as reflected in spreads. For instance, we know that in a normal market the July/March meal spread tends to have a 90-day window starting around the first of December through the end of February, where March meal loses to the July. Accordingly, we'll analyze that spread as early as late September, in order to formulate ideas about whether or not we're beginning to see some normal or unusual things develop in this year's grain market.

Q: Can you take me through a specific trade from the point of analysis all the way through the management of the trade so I can get a feel for exactly what your thought process and market actions look like?

Coy: I think a good example would be a trade that I believe is currently developing. It is now December of 1996 and the soybean meal market has been in a very strong uptrend since July of this year. It had a strong up move from a flat price of about $185 all the way up to $270. Then it backed off in keeping with the seasonal pattern where the lead month traded around $215. The meal spreads were running about even money, with the nearby months being at par value with the deferreds. If you remember, we were coming out of a year that had a relatively tight carry, not extremely tight historically, but nevertheless a market that had a 180 million bean carry out.

Coming up in the fall we had the potential drought in South America and you know it was going to be sensitive. Also, the Chinese, unexpectedly, for the first time ever, began to buy large quantities of U.S. meal, which further tightened the front end of the market. Of course, I was watching all this with a great deal of interest, knowing that the increased demand would cause a flat price to rally. At the same time all of this was developing, we had the second largest crop of record, a crop in excess of 2.4 billion, which was 200 million bushels more than was anticipated. The result of all this was that we began to see the spreads tighten; from early October to mid-December, the spread moved from even money to a $13 premium. During this time, there was a lot of talk in the industry that world grain demand had outstripped production capability; that the Chinese would change the world supply and demand balance forever. In my analysis, I respected what was going on, but said, "no way." Clearly, there was an expansion of demand but I knew we could fill these holes in the world demand for meal. I thought to myself, all we've got to do is harvest beans and run the plants and crush an average of 30 million tons a week. All this time the spreads were moving out to larger premiums. In the first week of December, we began to see some signs for the first time of availability, we began to see some competitive offers. We began to see some truck meal available. We began to see some things that indicated that I was right that the market had the ability to satisfy demand. At the time most traders were focusing on the technical strength of the spread. Sure, it looked great on the charts. I thought this was a terrific opportunity. And so I moved ahead and sold the spread. As I said earlier, I use fundamental information to identify a change in the market tone and direction. I put on a sizable position using this analysis. When I say I put on a sizable position, we bought 1,600 May/March spreads and 1,000 July/March meal spreads.

Q: In your analysis, the current premiums from the front to the back of the market are no longer justified. Is that right?

Coy: Exactly. During this period the spread differential had gone from full carry to a large premium.

Q: What is the carry price approximately?

Coy: Carry is roughly $3 a month, so it would be $6 full carry from March to May and $12 full carry from March to July. The potential of this trade is really huge—$1,000 on just one spread.

Q: You have described how you use fundamental information, but I know that you don't live in a fundamental vacuum. I know that you look at charts and other technical data on occasion.

Coy: More than occasionally!

Q: You have over 40 years of trading experience in the fundamentals of grains and have been very successful in your trading career. What would you say to people who have concentrated their efforts exclusively on the technical side of trading? Could the spreads that you have analyzed for me a moment ago have been identified by a trader using technical analysis?

Coy: I definitely believe so. What the technical trader has to do is devote himself to three or four markets and become expert in them. I'm absolutely convinced that spread traders need to focus on spread differentials exclusively. In my judgment you can't be successful trading 15 different commodities on a spread basis. You've got to decide on three or four commodities and dedicate a lot of time to understanding their peculiarities. The execution of spreads is a critical factor. You may be able to identify a market, but the spread has to be executed, both entry and exit, on a timely basis, because the windows of opportunity are often narrow. So you must learn to be expert in terms of your timing.

Markets don't stay at carry for too long if they're not apt to remain there. They can stay at discount for a time, but usually when they give up, they have a tendency to absolutely give up. It's not a half-hearted effort. If conditions change enough to have driven a spread from carry to premium, usually it's a long-term trend and you want to be on it when it starts to move.

When premiums evaporate they go much quicker, which is why the timing is so critical. You have to move faster with bear spreads than bull spreads because, unlike bull conditions that take months and months to develop, bear conditions such as the one I cited where I sold the front month premium develop very quickly and often it feels like if your timing isn't perfect you'll miss the trade. So again, you really need to focus on both execution and timing.

Q: What do you think are the advantages and disadvantages of spreading?

Coy: I think one of the disadvantages of spread trading is that you have a tendency to put on a much bigger position than if you were outright. Remember, it's possible to get into a spread where both ends go against you. It can be extremely painful financially. You have to be aware of the fact that spreading in and of itself is not a safety net. Spread trading is an effective means, no doubt, for managing risk. However, it's the inherent nature of the trader that I'm talking about: spreaders tend to carry very large positions. Also, I think the instant gratification is much greater in outright trading than it is in spread trading. You have to be a lot more patient when you trade spreads and realize that you're going to move up and down and that all spreads are going to have some drawdown. There's no such thing as a spread that has perfect seasonality. You have to remember that you can be right in a spread but you must allow for drawdowns in between, and again you certainly have to be vigilant about the size that you do. What I do when I go into a particular spread is build into my analysis the maximum drawdown that's ever occurred in that spread. I use that as a determinant for money management and position size.

You have to be careful in spreads, particularly if you're a market maker in spreads, as I am. When you exit, you've got to move rapidly. You've got to be decisive in what you do. There's only so much size can do effectively. And you have to come to some comfortable position that can be moved in the market without defeating your own purpose. You know, the spread market is really ballyhooed but you probably have to be more careful about size, if you're a large trader, than if you do outright trading. If you overstay your welcome in spreads, you can literally find that you don't have a market to liquidate your position. The spread turns and nobody wants to be on the other side of the price differential. So once again there's a timing element to me that's even more critical in spreads than in the outright market.

Q: Well, then, what are the advantages of spread trading?

Coy: I find that basically, other than commercials and professionals, there's not as much knowledge about spreads. As you know, spreading adds tremendous amounts of liquidity to the overall volume in all commodities. Most traders avoid using the spread market. They don't trade spreads and so I believe it is sort of a neglected area of the market. Consequently, spreads provide a huge opportunity!

Late in 1995 we saw the declining U.S. corn stocks, the declining world stocks of feed grains, period: corn, oats, rye, and barley. We saw them going down because of low prices and low production around the world. We "speculated" that we were going to end up with way too much demand for the supply and that there was a high probability that we were going to go down to an extremely tight carry. Accordingly, I moved into a spread that, based on my knowledge of the cash market, had to work. I bought September and sold December corn at 14 to 18 cents premium, which, at that point in time, the market was eager to sell to us. We put on 20 million bushels at that price differential. We sold the position out at an average of 62 cents.

Q: I think if we were to take a look at a chart of the September/December corn spread, we'd notice that the market gave a very clear buy signal, and once the trend was established, it was intact for a good period of time.

Coy: Absolutely. From my perspective, it was just a vivid example of following the cash market. You begin to see a picture unfolding that tells you that this year is a different sort of year. That's why I think, purely from a fundamental vantage point, you can identify situational patterns and if you know how to exploit them in spreads, the likelihood of you making money is much greater than an outright trade.

Q: Do you feel your approach helps in terms of dealing with the psychological barriers that typically prevent traders from being successful?

Coy: I think so. People who aren't successful with trading tend to want to catch every move in the market and in fact try to "beat" the market. Spread trading takes you out of that combative, adversarial psychological attitude about the market.

Q: I think spread trading not only forces you to be patient, but it also gives you a second look at the market, during periods of volatility.

Coy: I think that is exactly right. As a rule we don't get involved much in bear spreading. Most of our spreads are confined to bull spreading, to buying the nearby and selling the most distant month. This stems from the fact that the risk in absolute terms is circumscribed to the price of full carry where commercials will step in and take the physical product. From that standpoint, spreads are very much an advantage to a trader as opposed to an outright trade. Things can happen overnight—a crop report or government decision. Overnight the Chinese decided to grant an import license for the purchase of a million tons of soybean oil. They had never allowed imported oil before. All this is to say spreads provide terrific opportunity with reasonable risk. Also, I've found, particularly with bull spreads, you can sleep at night knowing you're not going to get blindsided. You're not going to take that tremendous hit that we all guard against!

Q: Do you think that spread traders have greater longevity in the market than outright traders?

Coy: When I look around and see who are the premier spread traders in the grain complex, many of them are the same players who were around 20 years ago. I can't say the same thing about outright traders.

Q: The turnover for outright market makers is much more rapid?

Coy: I'd say that for every good spreader who's on the trading floor, at least five outright traders have come and gone. I think there is a reason for that. For most traders, spreading lacks the energy and excitement of an outright position. Also, to be a successful spreader you really have to study the data, fundamental and technical. It requires hard work. Spread trading is a more complex game. And you really have to understand how to be patient.

Q: But it can be more consistent.

Coy: It can be a lot more consistent. There are many seasonal and cyclical spread opportunities that prove to be consistently profitable even in flat or trading range markets. You can have a static market that you can't make a dime in, that offers some real nice spread moves.

Q: What you're saying is that the market doesn't have to have a major move in order to have a significant spread relationship change.

Coy: In the grains, you can have a market that basically has a $5 trading range, say in meal, and you can have a spread that actually moves beyond the trading range because the tail end of production dominates the market. For instance, you can be involved in the March/July meal spread like we are now and have the front move $5 and the back move $5.

Q: The other way.

Coy: That's right—a $10 price differential move at a time when the market is essentially not doing anything.

Q: Which means you can have twice the move in the spread than you do in the outright market.

Coy: It happens all the time, which is why I continue to focus on spreading.

Q: What advice would you offer to someone who was just beginning to explore a spread trading approach?

Coy: Regarding the grain complex, the first thing I would do is find out where all the delivery points are and know exactly what are the premiums or discounts for purposes of delivery. Also, I would learn the intricacies of each listed grain contract. I'd study contract specifications and know the storage rates, whether it's meal or beans or corn or wheat. I would also learn what the fixed storage rates are and how interest is computed against the particular grain to come up with complete carrying charges. All this might sound elementary, but I find that a tremendous number of traders do not possess this kind of information. I think it is important to know how much it actually costs to take a barge of corn from Chicago to New Orleans. Remember, the corn contract is a vehicle for trading a real commodity. Sometimes traders lose sight of that fact.

I believe having this knowledge allows a trader to understand what conditions would cause the spread to move. All of which is to say you've got to have a good, sound understanding of the pure fundamentals that drive the market. This will allow you to identify a changing set of circumstances through cash basis or through freight rates.

In my opinion, technical analysis is not an adequate substitute for what I would call the salient statistics of the grain business. You need to know more facts about the market itself to trade spreads in order to be successful. I think you need this type of information for trading spreads. Perhaps, if you're an outright trader you can get by on technicals alone. If you're just spec trading and you're keying off on a 10-day moving average, or a 20-day moving average, the market crosses the average and you get long. Spread trading I do not believe is that simplistic. The spreads are fairly complicated, which means two things: you have to spend a lot of time on your analysis and when you're right you won't have a lot of company.

CHAPTER 7

John Newhouse

*John Newhouse is a member of the Chicago
Mercantile Exchange and owns a large
Eurodollar spread brokerage company.*

Q: How did you become a trader?

John: I was coaching little kids' football with John McGuire who, as you know, is a member of the exchange and like many traders on the floor was first introduced to the business through social contact. John convinced me to trade at the Chicago Board Options Exchange back in 1973. John wanted to buy a membership for investment purposes and he needed a body to be there, so I was that body! That is pretty much how I got involved with trading.

Q: What were your first trading experiences like?

John: As I said, I went to the CBOE in 1973 and started trading there for about two years. As you know, it was the first real options market. Back then, everyone used to sell premium, and by today's standards the prices were totally ridiculous. The exchange then gave you credit for any naked options you sold and didn't have any margin requirements. It took them about six months to figure out that something was wrong.

Q: Then what?

John: Well, when the Chicago Mercantile Exchange started the gold contract, John talked me into coming over and soliciting gold spread business. At the time no one was doing it and I thought it would be a real opportunity.

Q: At the CBOE, were you doing outright trading or were you spreading?

John: I was a market maker on the floor. In options, most strategies involved spreads, and that's how I really got interested in spreading. When this opportunity in gold spreads came along, I really was excited about it because spreading was something I felt I really understood.

At the CME I developed a spread business doing only spreads. I really believe that the spread market is kind of the glue that holds all of these markets together. Spreading was particularly good in the gold market because it was a cash-and-carry market, where the commercials were definitely interested in the spread relationships. Also, in the 70s it was legal for people to take delivery and create some beneficial tax situations by using the spread market.

Q: Were people making money trading gold spreads in the pit?

John: Yes.

Q: Was there enough in the spread movements at the time for off-floor people?

John: Yes, definitely.

Q: You're talking about gold, intermarket spreads, is that right?

John: Month by month. And you know, you've got two bangs there, because the spreads were influenced by the price level of gold, so you could set yourself up to be either long or short the price of gold. And at the time, prior to interest rate futures, you could actually use the spreads as an interest rate hedge, because they moved along with interest rates. And if you think back to those times, I think it was 1980 or '81 when the prime rate hit 17, 18 percent, there was really a lot of interest rate volatility. The gold spreads were a good way to hedge some of that volatility. It was unsophisticated but it was widely used at the time.

Q: John, how did these early experiences help you formulate what you're doing currently?

John: I really think that it gave me an approach to the market I'm currently trading, the Eurodollar market, that maybe is a bit more conservative in terms of price move expectations. As I sit down and analyze markets, the market can create spread strategies that will give me greater flexibility and psychological comfort than outright positions.

Q: So what you're saying is, it gives you the ability to manage risk better both financially and psychologically?

John: Yes.

Q: John, you specialize in Eurodollars. Do you need to become a yield curve expert in order to become a successful Eurodollar spreader?

John: I really don't think so. As you start getting a basic understanding of the spreads, you become aware of the characteristics and mechanics of this market. Basically, spread trading Euros comes down to anticipating what the Fed is going to do and when they're going to do it. From that perspective, the spreads are pretty predictable. I mean, you can predict with relatively strong reliability that if a particular scenario comes about what will happen to the Euro spreads. I think that makes it somewhat easier for people to participate in this market. If, for example, anticipating that the Fed will ease, you know that if they do, you're going to have a successful result in the spreads; and if they don't, you have a lot of options at your disposal in utilizing the spread differentials. In other words, you can take a position in the market based on what you think the future course of action is going to be and if it doesn't materialize within a particular frame, you can just spread a different option or series of option months. You know, it's really pretty predictable.

Q: Can you take me through a particular scenario that you might have formulated in your own mind? Just relate as best you can how you set up the trade based on whether, let's say, the Federal Reserve was going to ease or tighten monetary policy and just how you formulated your strategy.

John: Let's say that, as I'm looking at a particular market situation, the consensus is that interest rates are coming down and the Fed is going to ease. As I look at the implications of that effect, I see that it's going to price all markets out into the future at a little bit of a premium based on the introduction of the ease into the market. So I think both in terms of the overall result to the market and also the timing of the ease. Now if the action comes later than anticipated, the front month is going to converge down to the cash level as it expires; in other words, the fronts will lose to the backs. On the other hand, if the Fed's easing goes into effect immediately, the front months are going to gain the most, because that's where it's going to have the most impact.

Q: That's where the surprise will be!

John: Yes, and it requires an immediate price adjustment.

Q: So, you are looking for both the overall effect of monetary policy as well as the specific timing of when it will go into effect.

John: And you know, if you look at some of the Eurodollar spreads over time, you've got some tremendous moves. It really gets down to the basic function of our contract. You know, futures markets are designed to anticipate what prices will be in the future. Accordingly, the actions of the Fed have a major impact on price structure. It's amazing how efficiently sentiment is priced into the interest rate market. I mean, if the market thinks you're going to have just one final ease, if you look six months to a year out, in actuality, you lose premium. And yet, if the market thinks this is one of many eases to come, there'll be tremendous premiums placed a year out. Think of the spread relationship opportunities this presents to the trader!

Q: And of course, as we've seen recently, the market sentiment can be wrong.

John: Yes, but it does give you the ability to look at what the situation is today and ask, "Do I agree or disagree with it?" and take advantage of what the opportunity is right now. I mean, if you're absolutely against what the current consensus is, the Eurodollar spreads give you a tremendous advantage, because there are so many combinations of strategies that you can adopt to capture long- or short-term differential inefficiencies.

Q: In your opinion, what are the advantages of spreading Eurodollars as opposed to taking an outright position?

John: I think a lot of the advantage for me is that the price movements generally are smaller than the outrights. The spreads tend to move in a more steady, predictable pattern as opposed to the fluctuations of the outrights. And for someone who wants to have a longer term perspective of what the market is doing, the spread gives you protection to be in there. And of course, a huge advantage in Eurodollar spreads is the liquidity of the market.

Q: So in terms of execution, the slippage is really minimal.

John: Our markets are so thick that if someone wants to do a hundred-lot spread, it's nothing! Many times our customers will come in to hedge large portfolios and positions. Sometimes you'll see orders for 50,000 or 100,000 spreads and they can be executed without significantly affecting the market. It might take you a week, but they can really get these size positions moved. So liquidity is a real advantage to our market.

Q: Should an outside trader shy away from the Euro market if he only does a 10- or 20-lot spread size? Will his order be executed just as efficiently as the institutional trader?

John: I think the smaller orders are even more efficiently filled. They are very easy to do. The other big advantage for the smaller customer is, as these large institutions are rolling positions, they do put the spreads a little bit out of line. I think that opens up an awful lot of opportunities for people. They should be looking at rollover situations the same way that the local market makers do.

Q: From a psychological perspective, what would you say are the advantages of spread trading as opposed to taking a naked long or short market position?

John: I think the psychological implications of spread trading are very interesting. There is certainly a group of risk-averse traders who enjoy the security of the spread market. Based on this temperament or personality or just their general approach to the market, they look for trading strategies that have little day-to-day fluctuations that tend not to force them out like what might occur with an outright position. Spread trading also lengthens your ability to take another view of what you see in the market. If you're an exclusively outright trader you can run into a problem with being stopped out just because of some political statement or the release of one number.

Q: Alan Greenspan does have a habit of getting in the way.

John: Yes, and it can be a very temporary thing. Generally, the spreads, once they're moving in a trend, require an awful lot to get them to change direction. In addition, the band they move in is considerably tighter than the outright market. So the spread does afford the trader additional protection.

Q: Up to this point you have spoken about the Fed and monetary policy and, in other words, the fundamental factors that go into, let's call it a macroeconomic analysis of the market. What role in your trading does technical analysis play as you personally formulate your Eurodollar spread strategy?

John: For me, the technical aspects of the market are critical. You must know the outright market in terms of support levels, resistance levels, and general trends. You have to take all the technical factors into consideration when you do your analysis. Of course, I look at things fundamentally but I'm more concerned with the technicals of the spreads than the fundamentals on the floor. In fact, as far as fundamentals go, the floor trader is at a disadvantage. I don't think on the floor fundamental information is as good as it could be. I mean, we don't have the economic staffs that a large trading institution has.

And that is why I'm more concerned with technicals, because we are always judging market action in terms of what we see given the historical chart formations.

Q: So essentially you are saying the concept of trend is just as reliable for you on the floor as it is for the outright position trader who is trading in front of a screen?

John: Yes, that's right. I think if you look at the spread charts over time, you will see this to be true. If you go back and analyze, I believe it was 1994 when we went through a series of, I think, seven tightenings by the Fed. If you watch how the Euro spreads acted over an 18-month period, they were very consistent. The trend was very predictable. The market followed a consistent trend for 18 months in a row.

Q: It was a solid trend.

John: I think that is characteristic of this market. If you go back through the history of this contract, you will see the relationships in the spread continue for a long, long time.

Q: I think what you're saying suggests a very strong case for people to utilize spreading as a trading vehicle, not only in Eurodollars, but also in many of the other markets. As you know, I was a spread trader in the pit for many years in the ags and you're a spread trader in the Euros. I think the approach in spreading whatever market you're trading is fundamentally the same: identifying and capturing the differential. Do you think the approach of the outright trader is significantly different than that of the spreader in terms of identifying market trend?

John: The strategy might be different, but I think fundamentally, you have to make a decision as you're trading spreads about the general direction of the market. Once you make that determination, you can analyze the spreads accordingly. You can then begin to feel comfortable with the fact that the market is continuing in a particular pattern. Again, I think if you look at an historical chart of interest rates just for the short history of the Eurodollars you will see, during this 15- to 17-year period, four or five significant moves in the market.

Q: You mean long-term trend moves.

John: Yes. There was an increase in rates, followed by rates going down. Then rates went up and later reversed. This isn't something that changes every six weeks or so. These spread relationships are trends that are consistent and predictable. They do get a little volatile as you're changing direction, and that is why I feel you have to really pay attention to the market's technical areas. When historical areas of support and resistance start getting violated, it's a big warning signal that something's coming and the interest rate environment is changing.

Q: I should point out also that there is tremendous opportunity in the deferred months going out a year or two or more in the Euros. If you take a look at the movement in the back end, sometimes it is significantly greater than the movement up front. And there's also tremendous liquidity back there. The implication is that traders can get involved in a market that seems to be quiet in the present if they think there is a move materializing in the future. Even when the market gets very quiet up front there can be tremendous movement in the back months.

John: That's true. There's really a lot of opportunity on both ends of this market.

Q: There are also cyclical and seasonal patterns to be aware of in the Euro spreads. Isn't that right?

John: I think the biggest thing to be aware of in Eurodollars is that there is an end-of-year phenomenon where many companies want to window-dress positions in order to face-lift their balance sheets. And as such, there's a phenomenon called the end-of-the-year term, where you borrow money on the last business day of the current year with the intention of paying it back on the first business day of the next year so your published statement will look different. This becomes a very volatile phenomenon in the market. As you look back over the history of Eurodollar interest rates, this has a big impact on the December contract. It can cause it to have quite a bit of movement in relation to the yield curve, and it is specifically due to this end-of-the-year phenomenon. There have been times where interest rates might be at 5 percent and people are willing to pay significantly higher rates to borrow for that two-day period. And it's in times when funds are tight that you get some tremendous reactions in our market. The point is when you're trading the December Eurodollars you have to always be aware of this situation.

Q: Are there any other cyclical or seasonal factors that you are looking at when you formulate your spread-trading strategies?

John: You know, it's really funny, because when you get right down to it that's a recurring phenomenon that we deal with every year in the market. Other than that, my focus is primarily reacting to the monetary and fiscal policy of the government. I still believe the name of the game in the Euro market is predicting what the Fed is going to do, of course, having in mind again what the technicals are indicating as well.

Q: But in essence it's long-term Fed policy that you're looking at?

John: Yes.

Q: But in between Fed announcements, there's a lot going on in terms of the spread relationships.

John: Right. Again, I think the biggest thing in our market, if you look at it out six months to a year to five years, is that we're influenced by what the yield curve is doing, and of course this is all anticipation of the future. You know, you can go into a period like today where the consensus is that the Fed still has two or maybe even three more tightenings to come, and now we've rallied well over 100 points in our front month contract. But if you look at where the market is sitting in December of '96 in contrast to the December of '97 contract, the move is twice as much. There is your spread relationship! And what happened is, the consensus of two more tightenings caused the pricing to be taken out of the market. People are even talking now about maybe the economy slowing down; maybe the next Fed move will be an ease, and that's starting to engender market reaction. We've seen a tremendous flattening of the yield curve in the back, back six months to a year to two years. The deferred months are gaining significantly on the front. That's gone on for a good six months to a year now.

Q: What this all equates to me is opportunity.

John: Right. It is a tremendous opportunity.

Q: The Eurodollar market moved 100 points in the front months and 200 in the back; a good trend follower might have identified this as a good buying opportunity.

John: Right, and could have been adding the whole time. I'd say it's the absolute best market for that type of trader who has the ability to add to a winning position. When you look at these trends and how long they go for, if you get in at the right time you can continually add to your positions. The opportunity is truly phenomenal. And again, you can use stops to protect yourself.

Q: What Euro spreads are you looking at right now for yourself?

John: I'd say right now my interest is right up at the front end of the complex; the first three or four contracts. You're really seeing this idea that maybe things are going to be slowing down in the economy in the future. We saw for the first time in November that the November contract settled under the December. Now we're seeing the December under the March. The March/June spread is running around ten points premium. I would imagine you'll see that go negative, maybe even ten points negative. So you're talking about an interesting profit potential, particularly if you want to develop a fairly large position. It may take six to eight weeks to develop, but I think the market is heading in that direction.

Q: What is that situation telling us?

John: I think it's telling us that really people are losing a little bit of enthusiasm about the economy. That things might be slowing down and that the growth that we saw two quarters ago isn't going to keep up. If anything, the Fed might have a problem with keeping things going and will have to consider easing into the future.

Q: Do you think that spreaders, as a class of trader, have more longevity than position traders?

John: I think you and I are probably good examples of that!

Q: We're old guys, right?

John: I think as you look at the agricultural areas and you look at the interest rate areas, I think spreaders do tend to stick around for a long time. I don't think they make the gigantic money that some of the outright traders do, but it's a lot more consistent and predictable and the risk is much less and so is the volatility.

Q: What advice would you offer to somebody who is beginning to explore spread trading?

John: I think the thing that you have to really do is develop a game plan based on technical analysis and be disciplined about controlling risk. In other words, really believe your technical game plan, and when the market violates a level that you think it shouldn't, have the discipline to get out of the position and move on to the next trade.

Q: Just like any other good trade.

John: Right. The key is to focus on the differential in the spread and be disciplined.

I think traders go through periods where we're doing well, and alternatively we go through periods where we're having a hard time. We're just not in tune with the market. I think if you really analyze what you're doing, when you're doing well, it's probably that you're following the discipline of what you know you should be doing. All of us, myself included, when we run into trouble or have a tough time trading, it's generally because we haven't followed our discipline. You must get to a point where you can say, "I shouldn't let it go through this level; I'm wrong and I'm getting out!"

Yet so many times you hesitate or you rethink what you are doing and you don't follow the discipline you've set up ahead of time. I think it's almost like a football game. When you trade, you really have to have a game plan that is thought out ahead of time, and then you have to execute and follow it. And when something's going wrong, you've got to say, "Hey! It's going wrong. I didn't anticipate this, and this is all I wanted to risk, so I'm out."

Q: You have been around for a very long time and work and trade with the most successful spread traders on the exchange floor. In your opinion, is there any one thing that stands out that makes the best spread traders successful?

John: I think the biggest thing, when you really analyze it, is being disciplined and following your game plan. The best traders have set up risk parameters and they just always put the risk-reward factors in their favor. I don't care how good a trader you are, ultimately you need discipline to deal with profits and losses. How you deal with them will determine your ultimate outcome. If you keep your profits and let them run, and cut your losses, you're going to do very well. But there isn't anyone who can go in there and think, "Every trade I make is going to be right." It's how you react to situations that seduce you out of your discipline that makes all the difference in the world.

Q: If you had a final word to say to aspiring spread traders, what would you say?

John: I think the information flow is very good. Trading firms can give you the background of what's going on. You can set up a game plan, if you put in the time and effort. And again, if you have the discipline within yourself, you can be successful. It's like anything else! Except, I will say this, spread trading takes more work to come up with a game plan, but chances are that if your game plan is based on an inherently sound idea, its probability of working is much better than adopting an outright position.

CHAPTER 8

Girard Miller

*Girard Miller is a member of the Chicago Mercantile
Exchange and primarily spreads in the live cattle pit.*

Q: How did you decide to become a trader?

Girard: This goes back to 1969. I was trading and initially
had some successful trades but ultimately the profits quickly
disappeared. However, I decided I really wanted to approach
trading in a serious way. I came down on the floor of the
exchange and made up my mind that I would trade for a living.
Eventually I bought a membership.

Q: What were you doing before that?

Girard: I'm a CPA, and at that time I was a controller of a
marketing company. I happened to have my office right around
the corner from the old Mercantile Exchange.

Q: When it was still on Franklin Street?

Girard: Exactly, on Franklin Street. I'd come over often and
watch the trading. I felt it was really fascinating. And that's
when I realized, hell, I could make as good a living at the
exchange as I could managing a company. And I met a trader by
the name of Charlie Ponoroff who was very helpful.

Just when I started, memberships seemed to go sky-high. They went from $50,000 to $95,000, which put me out of the ballpark! When they dropped under $50,000, I called up Charlie, who told me that it was a good time to buy. So I bought an exchange membership. In truth, at the time, I really didn't know what I was doing.

Q: Girard, do you think your background as a CPA ensured your success as a trader because of your facility with numbers?

Girard: Possibly, but if you look around at who trades successfully, it really has nothing to do with being good with numbers. Look at all the market makers on the floor. Every profession and occupation is represented down here, you know, from an accountant, to a lawyer, to neurosurgeons. There are probably also construction workers who stopped digging pits and decided to trade, so it's not a measure of one's facility with numbers. There are other critical factors, which you have written about, that are essential for successful trading.

Q: What were some of your initial trading experiences like?

Girard: When I first came on the trading floor, I stood in the belly pit and traded outright positions, but I wasn't very successful. I remember at the time there was another member—he was also a CPA—after the market one day, we started to talk. It turned out that I went long and he went short, and we both lost money. And neither of us could understand why! In time, experiences like that gave you a little insight into how the markets worked and how you had to operate. I began to realize that there must be more to trading the market than just going one way or the other. In any case, it wasn't until I started working with a guy who passed away recently, Eugene Mueller, that I really understood how to trade the market. Gene was a spread broker and from time to time he would give me spread orders to fill. I had moved from the bellies into the cattle pit and they needed someone to fill orders in the back months. It was before the tax legislation was passed and the pack months did a very active spread business. So I started to do those spreads, and Gene Mueller and I worked together. He ultimately gave up filling orders back in the late '70s or early '80s and then I had the whole spread deck, and that's what I have been concentrating on for the last 25 years. I rarely ever take naked long or short positions in the market. I use a spread relationship as a vehicle determining whether I want to be long or short, or which month of the pair I think will move directionally more rapidly and with what kind of volatility. So in a way the strategy has a lot more complexity to it than just going long or short.

Q: Girard, can you remember any specific trade that would be of interest in your initial spread-trading experience?

Girard: Yes. I always remember one spread that I did. I guess I was filling an order. It was an intermarket belly/hog spread order. And I guess I made a mistake. I ended up with this gigantic position that went against me by thousands of dollars. I went into denial and I just left it in the account until the pain got to be too much and I got out. I always remembered after that never to spread positions that you do not have control over. And also never to spread positions that have excessive volatility. What this experience really did was make me learn how to pay attention to all the specific aspects of trading that you need to be aware of. In short, it taught me the need to be disciplined.

You see, experiences like that give you insight into the whole process of trading. It made me realize the rationale behind spreading as opposed to taking an outright position. When I took a naked position, I was subject to the immediate fluctuation of the market, so if I decided to go long and suddenly the market falls away 50 points, I'm going to have to get right out because I don't like sitting with a loss. When you spread, I found that you can sort of take a deep breath, and it doesn't mean that the spread's not going to go against you. It can, just as easily as an outright position, but it's not necessary for you to react as quickly as it is when you're sitting with a long or short position. What I'm saying is you get the opportunity to take an additional look. For example, usually if one month starts falling away, the other month's going to go down too. You have a little more time to make a decision. It doesn't mean you're going to be okay. I mean, you may still lose money, but you're maybe not going to lose as much and you will have an opportunity to lift one leg or ratio the spread directionally if you want to.

Q: That's what Bob Koppel says. The spread gives you a second look!

Girard: Absolutely. You can take a second look and a second breath!

Q: Could you talk a little bit more about how these early market experiences helped you to formulate your current market approach?

Girard: When I first got together with Gene Mueller, we used to have a method of evaluating the market. He had bar charts with single line closings that took into consideration at least ten years of spread relationships. Each year was a different color, and every day we would analyze the chart. What we saw was really amazing. Mind you, this was all done before the use of computers! We would see there were certain periods of time when maybe five out of six years the market went in a particular direction for five or six days. And we would put the spreads on regardless of what the market price was. The essential point was the differential. It could have been a 500-point differential. It could have been minus five. The point was that in that particular time frame, the market acted again and again in a particular way. We were very successful with this. It was almost a no-brainer! The worst that'd happen, you'd break even. But you see, this was a long time ago. Today, the markets work differently because the whole marketplace has changed. It's not only the economics of it, but the way the market is put together by the people who have control of the market. I shouldn't say *control* the market; what I mean is by the many different people who *use* the market. Today you only have about two or three large packing houses in the cattle market and the fund money changes the entire dynamics of the market as well. It's a whole different ballgame. You can follow trends, but they're not as meaningful as they used to be. Of course, you've got to remember, when I started trading the livestock market, it was new. A lot of techniques and strategies that worked when the markets were immature do not work today with the same degree of reliability because of the sophistication of the current players.

Q: I remember trading the cattle market in the 1970s, going away on a vacation with a large cattle position and the market didn't move 15 points a day. If you got a 25-point move in a day, it was a huge move.

Girard: That's right. Of course, then cattle was 28 cents.

Q: Do you confine your spread trading exclusively to the cattle or do you trade other markets?

Girard: Once in a while I'll do spreads in other markets. For example, Eurodollars and when the market was liquid I used to trade Treasury bills, but I would have to say the majority of my trading is still in the cattle market. I find it a very good spreading market.

Q: Do you use fundamental analysis in your trading approach?

Girard: No I don't and really have never concentrated on fundamentals because there is too much information to be gathered and no one can get all the fundamentals. It's just my own opinion. Also, if you're a fundamentalist you've got to adopt long-term positions. It's just something I've never been able to do. So I look at the market technically. I have found with the cattle market, you've got a relative strength spread. You don't have a carrying charge spread. The implication is that you need to understand the price action and volatility of each of the months you are trading as opposed to watching the spread itself.

Q: When you say relative strength, do you mean directional price movement?

Girard: Unlike the grains, there's no carrying charge to the cattle market so the spread itself is not that significant.

Q: So would you say most of the time, if the market is bullish and going up, the front month is leading the way?

Girard: Not necessarily. In fact, the commercials say if the backs don't lead the front on a bull market, you won't have a long-term bull market.

You see, because you don't have a market with a built-in carrying charge, there's no way to judge the differential between the two months, so all you really have, in my opinion, is the relative strength of each option. One is either stronger or weaker. If you look at each individually, you might find, technically, that one market looks a hell of a lot weaker than another market. And also there's the delivery times that you need to pay attention to. The fact that funds are involved, and they have to get out, has become a very significant factor. Of course, remember, the market doesn't always take the direction of the rolling over. In other words, just because funds are rolling out of the front doesn't mean that the second month will gain. What I'm saying is to be an effective spreader you have to have a sense of the entire market and really understand what is going on.

Q: Specifically, if you feel one month is acting stronger, you will buy that market and stay in that direction. Is that correct?

Girard: That's right.

Q: And is this on a daily basis, or does it take place over several days or weeks?

Girard: Well, currently I've been trading on a daily basis, but of course at times I do take positions. I used to take much larger positions and just sit, because the market trended. Right now the market isn't trending and I'm forced to make modifications in my general approach. In today's environment, just when you think you've got the right differential, it's not there anymore. So you have to be very careful and trade with a time frame that is working for you.

Q: Basically, what you are doing is looking at the relative strength of each month, but not the direction necessarily of the general market.

Girard: That's right.

Q: Can you walk me through a current spread trade or one that happened in the recent past just to give me a sense of your thought process—how you perceived the opportunity and what action you took in the market?

Girard: Well, very simply, I used to be very much inclined to forward spread as we approached the delivery month. I did this because over many years in observing what was happening, I usually saw that the front month would firm up around delivery time or just before first notice. And so I would routinely buy the front month and sell the next two months against it. There were some really large moves. It was not unusual to get 150 points on a spread within a week or two. Well, this was a lot of money for spreads. When you spotted these trends and got involved in these moves it was very profitable. And so I would attempt to identify these times and make that trade. In the last three or four years, it's been more difficult—the market has not consistently followed this historical pattern.

Q: We've been choppier, right?

Girard: Much choppier! It's just been an entirely different market. I haven't been able to identify the reasons, but I say who cares what the reason is, it's the reality of what you're trading that counts. I still would say, however, the beauty of trading spreads is that if you're careful you can maintain the capital. And even if you don't make large sums of money, if you're disciplined you won't lose a lot of money. And when you do hit it, you're going to get a good return. Whereas, my opinion is with a naked position for the amount of exposure you don't have as much opportunity.

Q: Outright positions are more difficult in terms of risk and money management?

Girard: Much more difficult. That's why, to me, spreading is really ideal. In fact, I don't know why more traders don't spread and why there are not more reps involved in the spread market for their clients.

Q: Do you mean retail brokers?

Girard: Yes. I mean, spreading maintains capital. I mean, that's the whole idea behind servicing your customer. They may not have as much upside, but you certainly can manage the risk. The client won't make 100 percent overnight on his market investment, but he can routinely make 10 to 15 percent.

Q: He hits singles instead of home runs.

Girard: Exactly. I would like to say that the fears or disadvantages to spread trading that people often express, in my opinion, are unfounded. They say with spreads you've got two months to worry about instead of one. Well, that's true to a certain extent, but learning how to handle two different months also presents opportunity. The worst thing you can do is waver between, are you going to spread or are you not going to spread? I think this is a simpler but very important point. If you're going to be a spreader, you must focus only on the differential. You can't hesitate after you buy one month and wait to sell another. That's when you get into trouble. You must determine from the outset whether this is an outright or spread position.

Q: It has been my experience that traders who are trying to avoid realizing their loss often will go into a second month. All they've accomplished in reality is to increase their vulnerability because the other month can go against them as well. So instead of wanting to see that loss in their account, they "fool" themselves into believing that they are spread.

Girard: And now they have two worries.

Q: Yes. Two worries and two commissions! In fact they now have two different trades, losers I might add, whereas if they had put on the trade as a spread because they were focusing on the differential, they would have had an identified opportunity over which they had control.

Girard: That's right.

Q: Do you think that the concept of spread trading makes a difference in terms of the psychological aspects of trading? Do you think spreading helps people deal with some of the usual psychological barriers?

Girard: What do you mean by "psychological barriers"?

Q: For example, a lot of people have trouble getting into a position and then taking it off.

Girard: Taking losses?

Q: Taking losses, getting into a position, pulling the trigger. And once they're in a position, they have trouble maintaining the position and all those kind of issues.

Girard: That's very interesting and as I was saying if you're going to be a spread trader, all you do is trade the differential. You don't even look at the outright market necessarily. Many times at the end of a trading day I don't even remember whether the market was up or down. But I can always tell you what the spread was doing!

Very often I don't even remember the settlements. I just know what the differential was, and that's all I'm really concerned with. I will tell you, in other commodities, it's the same thing, because there are some really tremendous opportunities, but I believe you've got to seize those opportunities with spreads. I always think in terms of the differential. That's what I'm trading. Whether it's cattle or hogs or Euros or anything else!

Q: Do you think that the spread trader approaches the market fundamentally differently than an outright trader?

Girard: Yes I do, because you're looking at relationships as opposed to the actual fundamentals of supply and demand. Of course you also naturally adopt an opinion of whether the market's going to be going up or down. You're really looking at the relationship inside (intramarket) and outside (intermarket) of the market all the time. Is April going to be better than February? Is February going to be worse than June? Often the relative strength of the spread can be an indicator of which way to go in the general market as the technical indicators would be. It is not perfect by any means, but you know, it gives you something to think about when you're trading.

Q: Earlier you mentioned your approach at delivery times. In your spread trading is there any seasonality to the trades that you put on for yourself?

Girard: Frankly, given my current style I can't identify them, because as I look at the charts that I'm now using the seasonality is not a big factor.

I can't tell you that this month is always better than the other month or vice versa. Of course many traders have exactly the opposite approach. They will point to certain months at different times of the cycle and indicate strong seasonality. As I said, it doesn't work for me.

Q: Is that because your time frame is relatively small?

Girard: Yes.

Q: And again, it's because you're looking for spreads. Well, you are looking at the relative strength of two months to determine the next day or two's move.

Girard: Of course you can successfully adopt a more long-term approach, which is what I would recommend for anyone off-floor. You will have to sit through some reversals, but if you analyze the differential well you can be quite profitable.

Q: What did you trade today?

Girard: I've been trading the February-April cattle spread.

Q: The February has been gaining?

Girard: In general yes, but it lost a little yesterday.

Q: But it looks like it gained it back today.

Girard: That's true, it did gain most of it back.

Q: This is a good example. Today, the Feb gained 17 points on the April, and yesterday it lost about the same thing.

Girard: Twenty.

Q: Right, 20 points.

Girard: I just happen to know. (Laughs)

Q: Lucky guess!

Girard: Right, I've been making lucky guesses for 25 years.

Q: So here we have two days where you might say we had no direction.

Girard: That's right.

Q: No relative strength.

Girard: Well, the way I see relative strength is a little different. When I looked at the spreads over the weekend, it appeared to me that the Feb was spiking up and was ready to be sold. So I came in on Monday morning and said to myself, "buy the April."

Q: And sell the Feb.

Girard: That's right, go short the Feb.

Q: Because you felt the market had gone too far for the moment.

Girard: Yes, I was looking for a temporary correction. I immediately saw I was wrong and got out, reversed, and went forward. It was working fine. It gained a little bit right off the bat and I'd say within a few minutes the spread reversed and moved from 90 to 125 points.

Q: A 35-point move against you.

Girard: Thirty-five points, and why? Because somebody came in and sold the February option at the close. There was no chance for any kind of recovery of the spread and that's the way the market closed. We lost 20 points. All within two minutes!

Q: And today, the pressure was not on the front.

Girard: The spread gained back about ten points on the opening and was that way all day long.

Q: The spread never did anything but make that initial gain.

Girard: Right, and then on the close it picked up another five points. In essence this is the way it goes day to day unless you catch a big trend.

Q: Do you find that the early part of the day generally sets the tone for the rest of the day?

Girard: What is more important is what happened the day before. But I must say in general you just have to trade the market; you can't get rules like that. Those sort of rules in my experience just don't work.

Q: Do you think that spreaders have greater longevity than outright traders?

Girard: Yes, I do. I think that the market makers on the floor with the greatest longevity are the spread traders. They're not as vulnerable to news or unusual events as are outright traders. You can still lose a lot of money, though. The reason you lose money is because you think you don't have as much risk; you put on a larger position than you should. In other words, where you might trade 20 or 30 outright, you trade 150 spreads. For a period of time it looks like the differential is moving ten points one way or the other and then out of the blue you get a tremendous move.

Q: It's a 50-point move—

Girard: It's a 50-point move or a 100-point move!

Q: When it goes your way, it's wonderful.

Girard: Yeah, but when it's unexpected in my experience, rarely is it profitable. And you see it's easy to get lulled into a big position. For example, for an exchange member there is no margin requirement for spreads. The position is marked to the market. So you asked before about the psychological aspects and I would say this is definitely an issue that needs to be considered.

Q: What advice would you give to somebody who was looking to become a spread trader?

Girard: I would say, learn how to identify the relative strength of each market by month and just start trading. Get a feel for the market, because there's really no way that you can instruct somebody about trading. You need the actual real-time experience. And focus on the differential at all times. If it's a carrying charge spread, figure out what the carrying charges are and base your trading decisions accordingly. With a carrying charge spread, if you know how far away you are from full carry, then you have something. One spread I never did, which I should have done, is the long bond spread. At one point last year, the long bond was 600 points above the short-term note. It was a perfect spread to buy.

Q: It has come in considerably. Now it's about 300.

Girard: It was out to 400-and-something just two days ago, but I mean, that was a great opportunity. That's something where you can watch a spread and really have an opinion.

I mean if you have a feeling about interest rates, it's a perfect way to trade.

Q: What would you say are the three most important factors for success in spread trading?

Girard: Discipline, confidence, and focus. Trading is trading. As I said before, the only difference between my style of trading and outright positions is I just trade differentials and am totally focused on that fact all the time. It's still trading!

Q: Could you say a little more about the role of focus in terms of spread trading?

Girard: You have to focus on what we've been talking about, the differentials. That's what distinguishes the spreader from all other traders, but the bottom line is, you must be disciplined. You've got to recognize when you're wrong or right and act confidently. The key is to be able to come back tomorrow.

I would just say to anybody who wants to trade spreads that the biggest failing of most people is that they don't understand what a spread really is and that is why I kept speaking of the importance of the relative strength of a market at any one point in time. You must understand the relationship and know one month is going to act better than another. So you just have to watch and make that determination. And one more thing—you can only do it by doing it!

CHAPTER 9

Steve Moore

Steve Moore is the president of Moore Research Center, Inc.,
a research firm devoted to seasonal research.

Q: How did you get interested in trading, Steve?

Steve: I was working for a lumber firm, and we were taking the actual delivery of plywood based on futures contracts. I saw the tremendous differences in price between the cash markets and the futures markets and felt that this was an area I wanted to learn more about.

This was in 1972, when there was a tremendous amount of market movement.

Q: So you were actually a hedging operation. Is that right?

Steve: Yes. We were eventually bought by a Merrill Lynch company. We were purchasing lumber and plywood for Merrill around the country. It was very exciting. That was right at the beginning of computers. We did a lot of regression analysis, things of that nature to look for, where prices were out of line—we would buy or sell lumber or plywood futures for hedging purposes.

Q: It sounds like a good foundation to learn about the basis.

Steve: Yes. I was really lucky to have had that experience. Then in 1978 I moved to my father's lumber company and set up a hedging futures operation. We got to trade through those very exciting, volatile late '70s markets when the gold, silver, and lumber futures markets were going crazy. We caught the downside of those moves from the very high interest rates.

Q: You mentioned gold and silver: So you were trading other things than lumber and plywood for hedging purposes?

Steve: Well, we speculated. We traded a lot of spec accounts through myself and the partners involved in the company. At one time we had 80 percent of the short open interest in the plywood futures contract. Essentially, though, we were primarily trading plywood and then lumber futures. But I did a lot of computer programming from the very beginning of computers. So we were tracking all the futures markets.

Q: What were some of your early trading experiences like?

Steve: Well, I can think of one thing that happened to us. We were hedgers, as I said before, and we were trading plywood futures when the price went up to $2.40 a thousand, which was an all-time high. When the price started coming down, we were quite short as a firm. The public and all of the experts kept saying the price was too low—below the cost of production, which meant to them, the price had to go back up. Everybody just kept buying the market. On the other hand, our company was very firm in our beliefs that the market was going to go down. And the one thing I learned, and I see people making this mistake all the time, is that there's no such thing as the cost of production when you're talking about a commodity. If there's one more buyer that's available for sale, then the price has to go up to take care of that buyer. If there's one more seller than buyer, then the price has to go down. And what happened in the plywood futures was that the cost of production readjusted. The July plywood futures, which had a high of around $2.40—went all the way down to a low of $1.58.

Q: The cost of production didn't stop the market from crashing.

Steve: No, the cost of production merely readjusted. That's what you constantly see happening in the grains and the meats. So many of the analysts like to quote a break-even point when they talk about pricing. There's no bigger mistake, in my opinion, of trying to determine price structure based on the cost of production.

Q: Steve, your firm, Moore Research Center is now the pre-eminent seasonal spread research center and historical spread service in the country. Were you using spreads when you traded the lumber market commercially?

Steve: Oh, sure. In the lumber market the spreading was huge. There was a particular trader who's a legend in the market. I'm sure you know of him. His name is Joe Siegel. He used to stand in the lumber pit, and he intuitively knew where all the spread values should be. He took on everybody, and I learned so much about spreads from just watching him. That man would take on hundreds of contracts. He would spread off everything. He never really traded a large outright position, but when it came to spreads, he would do almost any number. He made the lumber market a huge market. It has never been the same since his departure. He could figure out a way to spread off almost any order that came into the pit.

You asked me about how we were using the lumber market. Essentially, we were spreading to capture the seasonality of the market. Let me explain: The general nature of the lumber market is that most of the building is done in the spring and the summer months with a flurry of activity to conclude building before the winter weather sets in. Consequently, the production is pretty constant year to year. Lumber is an anticipatory market and so typically the lows in price, believe it or not, are seen in November. Typically the market rallies until about February 15th and normally establishes the highs for the year. Of course, this is the time just before the building takes off. As you can observe, the lumber market, because it is anticipatory, is just the opposite of what people would normally think. Most people think everybody's going to be buying wood for the spring. That's just not the case. When the trucks are moving, and the business is at the greatest demand, that's when the big wholesalers are actually liquidating inventories. They're not rebuying from the mills. They've already bought. They bought back in November and December.

Q: And this was reflected in the spread relationships in the different months?

Steve: Oh, sure. I know you've looked at the Merc's Goldman Sachs index, which has become so successful. What the Goldman Sachs people found many years ago, is there's a number of commodities futures contracts that exhibit a great degree of backwardation. Based on that observation they put together a huge fund. Those particular contracts are primarily the oil complex, the cattle, and the hogs. Now lumber is not a really liquid futures contract today, so it's not in there. Typically, backwardation means the front will trade at a premium to the back months. Probably your most classic example is if you look at crude oil on any given day. Almost always the front is at a premium to the back months. Therefore, extremely good spread opportunities exist for an individual or institution such as the Goldman people who are constantly buying the front of the market, staying with it and then selling it into the next month, constantly rolling the positions forward.

Q: Do you find these backwardations tend to increase as the cycle of the contract goes on?

Steve: In the oil complex, a couple of seasonals take place. One is in the heating oil, which is a fairly big market. The lows for heating oil futures typically take place around July 15th; after that, the market typically moves higher until mid-December, and that's when you pretty much get out of your longs.

Q: Like the lumber, that would be kind of anticipatory too, wouldn't it?

Steve: Totally. And then we've got a seasonal sell on heating oil in mid-January, which has been historically an excellent trade. What happens is, the weather usually gets real cold, and they put those final little rallies in the market. It's the public buying the heating oil futures up at the contract highs. But what you start to look at is—and I'm looking at it right now on my screen—we have closed front-month February heating oil today at 73.60. The second month, April, is at 67.80. That's a heck of a discount for just a two-month period.

Q: Do you find that if the seasonal starts to work, the spread will narrow in? Would you recommend selling February and buying April?

Steve: It's very dangerous, because you get into the delivery period. It's something that commercials can look at because they can stay in there until the last days of the contract, but that's not the type of trade that is advisable for the public. Where it would have been good was three or four months ago, if they had anticipated that as you approach this time of year, the February would trade to a large premium to the back months. In which case they would be looking to take the spread off somewhere in here. The cattle has always been excellent for spreading. More often than not, however, it has been hedger's nightmare because the front typically trades at a premium to the back months. So commercials are lifting their hedges and trying to roll them back. Consequently they are almost always having to sell at a discount; whereas the people who are the long hedgers, Goldman Sachs' approach, typically are able to sell out the front contract month and then go back and buy the deferreds at a discount. So that's the backwardation aspect of it. Today the spot month in cattle is a 60-point premium. That's not bad to be able to pick up 60 cents in one month. And as you know, every once in a while, you get some substantial premiums, 200 to 300 points between the first and second months.

We saw the same thing in the grains last year, where the really astute spreaders made just a phenomenal amount of money, because there was a bull market going on in grains, and they put their long positions in the front and hedged themselves by selling the back. The fronts just went to tremendous premiums.

Q: How did your early experiences in the lumber markets help you to formulate your current market approach?

Steve: The biggest thing that I've learned is that you should really do your research and look at the markets and not be dependent on other people to put together all the fundamental facts on what the market's doing. What I've seen for probably 25 years is that the majority analysts are almost always bullish at the top, and they're almost always bearish at the bottom. And I just don't want to fall into that category where I'm dependent on other peoples' analysis on a market. I've just found that you need to do your own homework to be able to succeed.

Q: Your homework is primarily technical, based on your computer studies of high probability trades in various markets. Is that right?

Steve: We've found that there are normal seasonal patterns to markets. The seasonal patterns exist in the grains. They exist in the currencies to a certain extent but are not as highly seasonal; what we have discovered is that there is a very seasonal nature in the financials because of the continuous operations of the U.S. Treasury, the way it keeps having to borrow money on a regular calendar basis. I'm more interested in what the price is doing, rather than in what people think the price should be doing based on the fundamentals. I can almost always show you a case at the top of a market where the fundamental argument declared that the market should have gone up substantially. In fact, at the top, the market had already gone up substantially. It had already anticipated all of that fundamental news, and that is what the seasonal analysis allows us to uncover. Look at the grain markets last summer! That was a perfect example. And if you remember, the spreads acted consistent with the historical patterns. Look at the soybeans against the wheat. The seasonals just made an unbelievable amount of money. The soybeans went down in the normal time window, and the wheat went sideways to up a little bit.

The soybeans and the corn are typically harvested in the fall. The majority of the wheat is harvested in the summer. Markets have a tendency, historically, to sell off into the harvest. But after the harvest there's usually a correction. That was the situation we had last year. Even though wheat was high last spring, the market really sold off very hard into the fall, and that's when the soybeans went down and the wheat went up.

Q: Specifically, what attracts you to spread trading?

Steve: The one thing that I've noticed over the years is that once a spread starts to exhibit strong directional characteristics, such as a bull spread, it continues a lot longer than one would anticipate. In other words, you normally don't have a bull spread for four or five days and then it's over. Normally spreads last for weeks or months in a direction.

Q: So you get very large trends in the spreads.

Steve: Correct.

Q: That's the way you basically have formulated your methodology.

Steve: As you know, we run correlation studies and the probability of the spread following a certain scenario just seems to work very well. It's probably related to what we were discussing before, for example with backwardation. There's just a very strong underlying spread differential characteristic in a number of our markets.

One of the more exciting seasonal trades that we've published for years is the pork belly and hog spread. Those particular trades have been very seasonal over the years, and I'm sure you could be telling me the fundamental reasons why those particular spreads work, but again, I've seen a number of years where trading long hogs, short bellies could be much more profitable than trying to take an outright position on either contract. In fact, there's been a number of years where you would have won on both sides of the spread.

Q: There's definitely a cyclical nature to the use of pork bellies as opposed to hogs. I think even with the advent of the new lean hog contract, those differentials will continue to be reflected in the spread.

Steve: I think you're right. Again, the meats are just excellent for spreads. There's a lot of liquidity and an actively quoted spread market. Most of the time you can ask your broker what the spread is like in the cattle, and they'll go into the pit, and they'll give you an immediate bid and offer. I also like spreading in the crude. There's quite a bit of movement in that market over time. Typically, when the market's going up, the front will gain a lot faster than the back, and when the market's going down, the front will lose a lot faster as well. All of which is to say there's a lot of movement in those spreads over the long term, so trading them as a spread can be extremely profitable.

Q: Can you take me through a current spread trade that you did recently?

Steve: I'll give you one that had a drawdown so people can see that spread trading doesn't always work! Our research found that bear spreading the June hogs, on approximately November 11th of every year, and holding it for approximately two months until January 10th, worked 14 out of the last 15 years as a strategy. That's where you're buying the back month and selling the front. What you're betting on is that the June is going to gain on the front. So this year that particular spread was entered at June approximately $1 under the February contract. And we might have been a little early this year, because like any trade you can never really catch the exact bottom day. This year the trade had a drawdown of about $600 marked to the market at year's end 1996. Then all of a sudden as we got up around the first of the year, we had our normal quarterly pig report, and as a result of that report the historical pattern kicked in. Today (January 8, 1997) the spread is trading June $1 over February.

Q: So there was a two cent move in the historical direction. ($800 profit)

Steve: That spread has actually moved three cents. It made another 40 cents today.

I do want to make one point very clear. When I look at a spread, I try to look at it as a trade with its own internal logic. In other words, if I'm looking at buying the June hogs and selling the February hogs, there's probably some reason that I think that the June hogs are going to gain on the February from a fundamental standpoint. Even though it is a spread relationship, I treat it as a hog trade. And if I'm looking to put it on at $1 under and take it off at $1 over, I'm just trading the relationship between the two as a strategy. But behind it all there is a fundamental judgment being made about the market.

Q: Do you think that spread traders have an advantage over outright traders when it comes to handling some of the psychological aspects of trading?

Steve: I think that really depends on the type of spreads that you're doing. It's one thing to be trading a front month, back month cattle spread where normally they will more or less move together. But if you take a currency spread, for example, Yen versus the Swiss Franc, psychologically, if you don't have a disciplined approach, you could actually lose on both sides of the spread for days, weeks, or months. It takes a totally different frame of mind to trade the intercommodity spread as opposed to the intracommodity spreads.

Q: That is a point well taken. Very often an intracommodity spread may have the same characteristics of two outright positions. That is where the research and discipline comes in.

Steve: Exactly, when you're dealing with two dissimilar entities like Yen and Swiss, it can become very difficult!

Q: Let's take a spread like the February/April cattle or the February/June hog spread. Is there any particular advantage for somebody to be looking at that kind of trade as opposed to buying or selling the February outright?

Steve: If you have studied the relationship between the two different contracts, you can see that there's some potential for it to move to another level, and if you can identify the risk, it can be a very lucrative trade.

Q: Do you think that somebody has a better chance of staying with a winning spread trade than they would with an outright position?

Steve: It's so much easier to stay with something that's winning than when it's not winning! But seriously, I think that's true.

The spread allows you to keep your position. It gets you in place for those kinds of events that can really make a spread go. Let's say you're bull spread the cattle. We know that is the normal tendency of the market, right? Suddenly you get into the month of January, and a cold front comes down through the Texas Panhandle. The market begins hearing about how the weather is killing thousands of cattle on the feed lots. Suddenly the cattle feeders are concerned that it's going to cost them a lot more to have to feed cattle. Those are the situations where the spread opportunities set up and suddenly you have the potential for the front months to put in substantial premiums over the back months. In fact there are many times that in these situations there is no impact on the distant contracts at all.

Q: Do you think the spreaders are more comfortable in volatile markets than outright traders?

Steve: As you know, many times being in the spread can provide more movement than the outright positions. You could potentially have the front months go up based on the cold weather and the back months actually going the opposite way. So these are the type of opportunities that get set up where people are overreacting to short-term events through the spreads. And that's the type of thing that I've seen where you've come in over the years and traded the spreads and knowing the seasonality of the spreads I think gives you the psychological comfort of remaining in the right direction.

What Moore Research Center does is basically use the computer to go back and study past history and find where, historically, the highest reliable trades have been and on that basis we offer opportunities for trades to take advantage of.

I do want to add one additional point. I study spreads whether I trade them as a spread or not, because if I go in and take an outright position on a futures contract, I need to know if I want to be trading in the first option, the second option, or the third option. Sometimes the opportunity is in only one option. Many times it could be in the third option only. If you're a hedger and you want to hedge your grain, and it happens to be in the month of April, odds are you should be hedging in the far back contract. Because if the market goes up in anticipation of a poor crop, typically the front will be the one that goes up. So just because you're not trading a spread, I think you still have to be very aware of what the spreads are doing and what they potentially could be doing in the future.

Q: I think that's an excellent point. I think that your example of the grains is right on target and even a speculator who is looking, let's say, to buy the market might take a look and see that one particular month is leading the way over the others. Why go into the weakest when you should be going into the strongest months?

Steve: If you came to me and said you were thinking about trading cattle, I would have to tell you that on any given day, I'm aware of what the first four contracts are doing relative to each other. If you're going to be a cattle trader, and you want to sell the market, you probably would not want to sell the front. You'd want to sell a deferred month for all the reasons I've already stated. It's very important for all traders, whether they trade spreads or not, to understand that the relationships change throughout time between the different contracts and profitable opportunities derive from an understanding of those relationships and price differentials.

I think it all comes down to this: You should not enter any trade unless you have a well-defined plan on what the market should do and also have a point at which you admit that it's not doing what you thought it was going to do and you get out. That can only come from studying the particular trades before you put them on, whether it's a spread or outright position.

There's got to be a reason that you want to buy a November soybean contract versus a July contract. You have to study and know your markets. You can't just observe a market, read the *Wall Street Journal,* buy the futures contract, or adopt a spread position.

Q: What words of advice would you give to aspiring spread traders?

Steve: The biggest thing would be to do your homework and study what the markets have done in the past so that when you get into these trades, you have a feeling of confidence in what you're doing, and you're not reacting to what the market's doing any particular moment of time. Learn to distinguish the signal from the noise.

And again, anytime you trade cattle or beans or oil, or even the financials, you have to decide which option would be best to be long or short. It gives you tremendous perspective on the market.

I think it was in 1985, the year of the drought. I had a client who bought the November beans in April because they were so much cheaper than the July beans. He did make a lot of money, but had he bought the old crop he would have made four or five times as much money. All of our studies at the time said a bull market, and indicated that you needed to be long the front month. So here was a situation where someone was trading a substantial outright position who didn't pay any attention to the spreads and, although he did make a significant sum of money, he could have made a heck of a lot more if he'd just done his homework!

CHAPTER 10

Margery Teller

Margery Teller is a member of the Chicago Mercantile Exchange and trades in the Eurodollar pit.

Q: How did you first get interested in trading?

Margery: I was recruited out of school. I worked for O'Connor and Associates, who were later taken over by a Swiss bank. I traded upstairs for about 14 months and then I went down to the exchange.

Q: Were you a clerk before you went down to the trading floor?

Margery: I was a clerk on the trading floor and then I went upstairs, where I worked on the trading desk, managing positions. Later I went back to the exchange floor to trade.

Q: And at that time, was it options or futures that you were trading?

Margery: Options. I traded options for about six years.

Q: Did your early experiences trading options influence the type of trading you are doing now?

Margery: It is almost exactly the same except there's no gamma risk–the same type of spread risks.

Q: So would you say then that your early options trading laid the groundwork for basically what you're doing now?

Margery: I think you have to know how to trade futures. Options and futures are two very different games. Futures trading is all momentum. Options trading is just knowing how to cover your rear the best you can.

Q: What made you move to the futures?

Margery: I saw the probability of the options side decreasing somewhere around 1990. The markets were getting too tight. I believe there are many more profit opportunities in the futures. The risk-to-reward is better in the futures. So I started to trade the rollover in the Eurodollars and eventually worked my way to the back end, where I now trade the last nine years out, 36 different contracts. What I'm doing is like a hybrid between options and futures.

Q: Could you talk about your current market approach?

Margery: What I do now is very simple. If I buy a particular contract month in Eurodollars, I'm going to sell something against it and then I'm going to try to profitably work out of the spread. I don't have a big risk approach to doing it. I don't ever think that I'm smarter than the market. If it doesn't work, then I'm going to get out.

Q: When you say you buy a particular month—

Margery: I try to buy it on the bid.

Q: You try to buy it on the bid and if you do, you're going to sell something else against it to lock in your edge?

Margery: Right. I mean, there's no real rocket science here. I just try to buy the bid and sell the offer. And if I can get the spread on at my price I think about ways to take it off.

Q: Well, it seems like a lot of hard work. Why spread trade at all?

Margery: Because spread trading is one of the most profitable ways to trade.

Q: Why?

Margery: Because a lot of people don't understand it. And in my opinion, it's also the only challenging game left. When you're trading Eurodollar futures outright in the front and let's say the market is five bid at six, there's no challenge in that. You buy fives, you try to sell sixes. When we're in the back, you have to figure out all the different price differentials. There may be seven different games going at once. If I do a trade, I know where I'm going with it. I have all the different contract months ranked in my mind. I'm thinking to myself, what is the best option, what's the second best option, what's the third?

Q: Can you take me through a trade that happened in the last few days or something that stands out recently?

Margery: Sure. Today, for example, I sold the five-year bundle. The five-year bundle is when you sell contracts for the first five years.

Q: You sell each contract in the first five years.

Margery: Right. I sold an 18-lot in a five-year bundle, which means I sell 18 in the front four and then I sell 18 in the reds, greens, blues, and golds. Each sequential year out in Eurodollars is color-coded (e.g., 1998 is referred to as "red"). So I sell 360 contracts. I made the market, I sold them down two and a half. The way you price things is you go against the previous day's settlement. So I sold them down two and a half ticks from yesterday's settlement. That's the average price of the whole thing. Now, once I did that, I had to decide what I wanted to spread against them. Of course, before I even made the trade I was considering all this. I know, in fact, that I wanted to buy the red June, which was the strongest contract on the board. So I made a market in the red June and I ended up paying down two for them, which I felt was really worth about a tick and a half better. At least a tick better than the five-year bundle.

Q: Did you cover all of the bundle in the red Junes?

Margery: Because I was short red Junes and essentially short the bundle, my top priority was to cover in the red June. If I didn't get them, I was going to buy the red packs, which would be buying all four red contracts. What I really thought I had to do was buy the reds. If I couldn't get the reds, I knew the back months were weaker, so I thought about greens, which were offered. If I couldn't get them, I could just keep going out in the market to the blues or even further back.

So, now I had several different ways to get out. And what happened was I got hit on my red June bid. So I didn't need the other escape routes.

Q: So you covered the entire bundle in the red Junes?

Margery: Exactly.

Q: What kind of market analysis made you put the bundle on in the first place?

Margery: Earlier in the day, Howard, I was able to buy the golds, which are the fifth year contracts out. They were absolutely killing the golds. So, in a way I had the bundle on the other way. I was long the five years down four and I sold the two-year down a half. To reverse, I sold the golds down two and a half and bought the reds down a half. Bottom line, I ended up locking in two ticks.

It doesn't often work out that well.

Q: What do you think are the advantages of spread trading?

Margery: Of course with the outright, you get to go home and you're flat. I mean, I go on vacation with the orange, blues, and golds.

If you are an outright trader, at the end of the day you can get flat. When I leave at the end of the day, I have position risk. As an outright trader, you don't have to deal with the huge margins! You get to go home and sleep at night. Of course, it is not as bad as options trading, where sometimes covering a losing position is out of your control.

Q: You have given me some significant disadvantages. What about the advantages of spread trading?

Margery: The advantage of spread trading is that there's a lot more edge in it. The reason I say that is because I have so many different strategy options. I can price any contract month about a quarter of a tick better than everybody else because I have all the different spread differentials to work with.

Q: That's because you're faster and smarter than your competition!

Margery: It's the fact that, because I have so much inventory and I know where I want to price everything, I can make a tighter market. It also allows me to trade considerably more than most of the other market makers in the pit.

Q: You mean in volume?

Margery: Yes, which means I don't have to make a lot of money on every trade. I can do it cheaper because of the size.

Q: You know, Marge, it reminds me of an old joke.

Margery: Which is?

Q: A manufacturer was asked about his margins and he said, "I lose a penny on every item, but I make up for it in volume."

Margery: Some days it's like that, I'll tell you.

Q: How do you think spreading helps you with the psychological considerations of trading?

Margery: Spreading is the trading vehicle that I use to maximize my profit potential with the least amount of risk. So to the extent that in a general way spreading addresses any of the myriad psychological issues that come up, it is perfectly suited for my unique style and personality.

I have to make one point very clear. I don't position trade. I don't make money from a directional bias of the spread going one way. I make my money from effectively getting in and getting out of the market. A lot of spreaders just say, the price differential is cheap and they put on the spread. I don't care what it should be.

Q: So you're basically scalping the different spreads and that is your main focus?

Margery: That's all I do.

Q: But you take spread positions home, don't you?

Margery: Oh, I have a huge inventory.

Q: And you just keep trading around the inventory?

Margery: Yes, I just keep trading around the inventory and look for intraday price inefficiencies so I can move in and out of the different contract months.

Q: Do you think the spread trader's approach to the market is fundamentally different from that of the outright trader?

Margery: Absolutely. I think outright traders are limited in the amount of options that they have available to them when they trade the market. On the floor, all the outright market makers want to do is get the edge. If you're an outright trader, all you're trying to do is sell the threes when it's three offer. It's a totally different mind-set! In my opinion, it's not really a thinking game if you're just trading one month. I come home exhausted every day because I am just thinking about all the different price differentials for six hours straight. I can't lose track of anything. I have to know where all the spread relationships are trading.

So I'm constantly making markets: primarily in three years, but I'm aware of different contract months. The ongoing challenge is to know where all the contract months are trading in relation to each other.

Q: Four years with four contract months a year?

Margery: Right.

Q: From the reds to the golds?

Margery: Of course, the liquidity decreases as you go back. The reds have been pretty tradable and the greens too are still reasonably liquid. From blues on back it is fairly illiquid.

Q: You spoke earlier about the five-year bundle and about the different component parts, for example, red packs and green packs. How do you price them?

Margery: You price them based on the net change on the day.

Q: With each individual contract?

Margery: You calculate a net change on the average of all the different contract months. So let's say I make a market on the green pack at two and one half. That would represent the average price of all the months within the green.

Q: So you would offer the whole thing at two and one half?

Margery: Yes. Now normally I'd say 90 percent of the time the different colors will go in a fairly smooth line. For example, if you have a big day where the spreads are moving, the reds might be down five and the greens might be down six, the blues and golds might be down seven. It's rare to have a day where the reds are down three, the greens are up one, the blues are down three and the golds are flat. It's very unusual for there to be an uplift like that. It happens occasionally, but I would say less than 10 percent of the time.

Q: Is there customer interest in the various packs as you've described them? Are there customers who are trading them for either speculative or hedging purposes?

Margery: I think they are used as a hedge against OTC trades.

Q: Do the orders actually come in as packs or pack spreads?

Margery: They do come in as pack spreads occasionally, but that's a very rare order. Most of the orders in the last eight years of the Eurodollars come in as packs. I'd say probably 60 percent of the greens trade as packs.

Q: So a customer order might do 100 gold packs.

Margery: Right. The order would read, sell 100 gold packs at a price or at the market.

Q: And then you make a market in all four contract months of the gold.

Margery: Right.

Q: And if the order read 100, that would mean—

Margery: Four hundred contracts.

Q: One hundred contracts times the four months.

Margery: Right—100 each month.

Q: That's really fascinating. Do you think the general public should trade these? Do you think they move enough?

Margery: Oh, they move!

Q: So there's opportunity for people who are looking at the various spread differentials in the back months of the Eurodollars?

Margery: Well there's certainly opportunity, but the margins are fairly high. They're not like S&P high, but they're high.

Q: So, if I traded a red against a green what would it cost?

Margery: Red against a green is okay. But, for example a red against a blue or gold.

Q: It's more costly because they're so wide apart?

Margery: Yes. I'm not exactly sure what the margin is. It's probably $400 a spread.

Q: That's really not too bad in terms of margin requirements for customers. The key point is, there is price movement, which of course translates into opportunity. How much can a red move against a blue?

Margery: Overnight?

Q: Well, over a period of days?

Margery: Twenty-five ticks. I mean, it's not huge but if you have a position on—

Q: That's pretty good. Could you speak about the role of discipline, confidence, and focus in your own trading?

Margery: Well let me think about the priority. I guess the first priority would have to be, you need to be confident in your markets. And in order to be confident in your markets, you have to know exactly what you want to do with the various spread differentials. Once I get a sense of the market based on the resting orders, I can make markets in any one of or all of 36 contract months. So the first thing I have to be able to do is make my markets with confidence, because if I'm going to make a market, I'll be good for at least 300 contracts either way, buy or sell. I have to be confident, and that has to come across because you don't get trades unless you show confidence and you are recognized by the order fillers. The discipline is obviously an essential aspect of what I do as well: If something starts going against you, you have to be able to get out. No questions asked! It is the golden rule of spread trading, any type of trading. And focus—if you lose your focus, you're kind of out of the ball game. You have to be on. I mean, I told you I come home exhausted every day. I have to be on every minute I'm in the pit. I probably make 1,000 markets a day! I'm probably making a quote every ten seconds. So I have to be completely in the game.

Q: It sounds exciting.

Margery: Well it is.

Q: What advice would you offer to someone who is looking to explore a spread-trading approach to the market?

Margery: I think it's more challenging and easier to spread trade.

Q: Why do you think it's easier?

Margery: Because you're not mired into one way of trading. It is hard, though, to teach somebody how to spread, because most people don't want to focus on more than one thing at a time. You can do it if you're off the floor, you know. It's quiet, you can think about it. I guess the first thing you have to teach somebody is how to price one thing off of something else. I've tried to teach many traders how to do this. You must know your markets and be able to adjust price differentials to changing markets. If the market turns on you, where are you going to sell? For example, you just have to know how to do that at all times. Sometimes I feel the challenge of spread trading is like walking across a tightrope with a sea of alligators waiting to snap you up.

Q: Really?

Margery: Because if you make one mistake in pricing, it could cost you big-time. So if you don't know where something is, you're buying blind. If I end up buying the worst green on the board, at some point, that's going to come back and bite me. That is where the discipline and focus kick in!

Q: Do you buy strength and sell weakness when you're spreading?

Margery: Always.

Q: Do you find that a lot of people have trouble doing that?

Margery: Yes, they do. They tend to fade the market and not follow the trend.

Q: Marge, do you find that the spreads in the back months of the Euros trend?

Margery: Yes, they do. When the tail starts wagging one way or the other, I'll just keep going in the direction of the trend. I still believe the old axiom is true: the trend is your friend.

The way our spreads move is that they tend to move with a correlation to the actual movement of the rates.

Q: Of course, anyone who is trading interest rates must be aware of interest rate movement and the yield curve.

Margery: If rates are going up, the spreads will react accordingly. For example, if there is upward pressure, the longer term rates are going to go up faster and I would get involved with spread differentials that are going with the trend. Once you learn your market and know the different spread differentials, it all gets down to what you were asking me about before and that is discipline, confidence, and focus.

CHAPTER 11

Jeffrey L. Silverman

Jeff Silverman is a member and director of the Chicago Mercantile Exchange. He is an active independent trader.

Q: How did you first get interested in trading?

Jeff: It goes back to a time in my life when I was very driven and trying to figure out what kind of career path I wanted to follow. I was in the seventh or eighth grade in Omaha, Nebraska. I was reading lots of biographies. I became particularly fascinated with the life story of Bernard Baruch, who was described as an arbitrageur, financier and adviser to presidents. That sounded like a pretty good job to me, particularly as a Jewish kid growing up in Omaha back in the 1950s. So I've always had an interest in trading, but I didn't know exactly how I was going to get to where I wanted to go. After I graduated from MIT, I elected to get directly involved in trading and make it my life's work.

Q: What were your early trading experiences like?

Jeff: The thing that stands out the most about my early trading experiences was my overtrading and overutilizing the leverage that futures allowed. One of the most attractive things about spreading was that you eliminated a lot of the random noise factors markets tend to have. I found I could enter positions in a less emotional manner. It's far easier to step into a crashing market and execute orders to buy spreads than it is to stick your hand in the fire and buy outright when there's no apparent bottom in sight.

Q: Were you spreading from early on in your career?

Jeff: From the earliest time I did some outright trading as well as spread trading. However, I should say in all, the studying that I was doing on the economic value of futures markets and analysis that I did on commodity prices focused on the relative value of one commodity to another. For example, wheat versus corn, or cattle versus hogs, or hogs versus pork bellies, or soybeans versus meal and oil. There was an economic rationale between all these spreads, both intermarket spreads and intramarket spreads. I was also interested in the delivery month of particular commodities and their relationship with the deferred months. I felt accurate pricing was conducive to rigorous economic analysis. And those differentials were easier to forecast than outright prices, because in my opinion, there was far less noise.

Q: You said something a moment ago that I thought was quite interesting. In a crashing market, spreads make it easier than trading outright to take a position. Is it the way you psychologically handle risk?

Jeff: Well, I think the comfort comes from the fact that you're able to reduce the risk while participating in the market. If you've plotted right, you can have the lion's share of the reward at less risk and less margin requirement. The more I thought about the concept of spreading or arbitrage and took it to its logical extreme, which is really relative value, then it became apparent that the concepts of spreading and relative value applied to all forms of speculation. Whether you buy one stock or another stock, it had to do with the relative value of stock versus cash, or stock versus bonds, or one particular class of assets versus another. I realized in some sense, everything is really a spread!

Q: In a sense, making the decision to buy one and not the other is really a price relationship.

Jeff: Cash and noncash is a spread relationship. So once you've started doing that kind of analysis, then everything becomes a spread, whether you considered it a spread or not, and that for me was a very liberating mental process.

Q: You mentioned that in your early trading experiences, you were quite volatile and overused the leverage.

Jeff: To an excess! It takes a while to develop some maturity and recognize that the minimum margin requirement that the exchange or the brokerage firm charges does not determine how large your position should be. And as simple as that may sound, it can take years to learn that lesson well, and some people never learn it! You know, the margin requirement at the Chicago Mercantile Exchange is directly related to the largest daily move in the course of a three-month period. So if you're going to utilize the full margin requirements to decide how big you're going to trade, the odds are you will go broke within the next 90-day period. That's the way the system is designed. Now, once you realize that, then you start using multiples of the margin requirement in order to avoid "risk of ruin."

Q: Were your early experiences with excess leverage primarily with outright positions?

Jeff: I was an equal opportunity, swing-for-the-fences kind of guy!

Q: Is there any one particular experience that stands out?

Jeff: Well, these are painful experiences. There were times when I went broke or was debit and had to claw my way back.

Q: I'm looking for the epiphany. I'm looking for that moment in time when you realized, hey! Instead of leveraging up and dialing it to the max, there is a better way.

Jeff: I wouldn't say there is any particular thing that I can point to. I just realized that the area in which I had a shortcoming was the money management. So I went out and proceeded to do what someone with a strong, scientifically based education does: I bought every book I could find on money management and read them and thought about them and considered how some other participants in the industry, notably Joel Greenberg, employed his money management strategies in the market. So this now is 1984, after trading for something like 16 years, I had this brilliant idea that I now was going to learn from my own mistakes. In addition, I was going to learn from watching other people's mistakes. I was explaining this strategy to a retired friend of mine, and he said, "Dummy! What do you care about mistakes? Look at what the smartest people are doing and emulate them." That seemed to me to be a pretty wise piece of advice, so I recast my net and started reading all the books I could about successful traders in order to understand what made them successful.

Q: What did you come up with?

Jeff: Successful trading, I think, is all involved in the search for "the edge." The edge meaning where you have some superior talent or some superior expertise that you can utilize successfully. You have to analyze yourself and know what your strengths and weaknesses are and do things that support that edge. Among the strengths that I have is a greater degree of patience. I'm very patient once I have a trade on. If I were to qualify my patience as to waiting until the right moment to enter a trade, that's another story. In truth, that's something I'm still wrestling with.

Q: You and a few others.

Jeff: Someone once said, "Don't diddle in the middle." Big money is made buying or selling at extremes. Extremes in valuation—extremes in people's belief about value is when you want to be acquiring a position, and looking for and knowing what the internal and external signals are that tell you you're near an opportunity point. This is crucial. If you look at trading analytically, there are several distinct aspects to a trading decision. What's the likely direction of the commodity? What's the appropriate time to enter and exit the position? And if you're talking about something that you may sit with for weeks, months, or even years, how do you express that trading position profitably in the market? Do you acquire a position in the nearby and continuously roll it as it approaches expiration, or do you selectively pick months in the far-outs that will give you enough time for your ideas to manifest themselves? In other words, markets go up or go down, but it's much more complicated to figure out the timing aspects, and consequently, for me, I spend a lot of my analysis focusing on and understanding timing variables.

Q: Could you give me a sense of your thought process as it relates to a current market that you're involved in ?

Jeff: One of the markets I'm currently looking at right now is the cattle market. The cattle market has some interesting aspects to it. It's got a very long economic cycle because of production variables. A cow has an eight- or ten-year life and similarly the industry cycle seems to have an eight- or ten-year life. I don't know if they're correlated, but if you go back over the history of the cattle market, we've had quoted prices back to the Civil War. There's been a tendency for cattle cycles from peak to trough to be somewhere between 8 and 13 years, and various factors cause the market to move, whether it's drought, or high grain prices, or what have you.

Now this past spring, as an example, we had a confluence of events. The largest total cattle herd, a drought in Texas and parts of the West, and extraordinarily high, in fact, record corn prices. Those events led to predictably low prices for feeder cattle. They led to distress selling of feeder cattle and cows and low prices for live cattle, which adds to the process of stimulating both domestic and foreign demand, so there are some good things coming from the cycle.

As we've increased the cow kill and stopped the withholding of breeding stock to replace the cows that are being slaughtered or dying, the cow herd fraction of the total cattle herd is being reduced, and the production of future animals that will come to market in 1998 and 1999 is being affected by decisions that were made as a result of economic distress in 1996. So one could rationally argue that sometime in the 1997 to 2000 time period, there's going to be a dramatic bull market in cattle, depending on inflation and the confluence of pork and broiler supplies, which are the major competing meats. There's a strong probability, in fact, that cattle prices will reach into the $80 to $90 area and feeder cattle could be $90 to $100. Those are kind of interesting numbers since, at the time of this interview, the cattle market is trading in the low $60s. So, you know, a $20 move could be $8,000 a contract. If you could catch this move in the front, and the spreads happen to go nearby month premium, you can roll them to the back and get a $2 or $3 discount every five monthly time period, and make an extra $6 to $12 a year because of the roll.

So, in essence, here's a perfect example. Prices are relatively low. The events that caused below-$60 prices in April of '96 are unlikely to happen again. We had a large supply and high corn prices that forced the feed lots to sell their cattle fast, and a drought that forced people to sell calves and feeder cattle and cows, and the demand was not yet built up. We know what the likely risk is. The market's probably not going below the lows that we saw in April of '96, and it's got the potential to go into the $80s.

Now the timing of this bull market will be a function of a lot of economic variables. In addition, a lot of early speculators who will pile into this thing on the hopes of things being great out in the future. And they may be too early, and they may end up selling their positions out at low prices, because they couldn't wait out the heat. And there might have to be a second round of speculators who will end up taking the position. There might be a third round of speculators before it ultimately goes. I've seen that before, too!

So to get back to my original point, it becomes a situation of study and timing. There's a lot of risk, and there's a big potential reward. If you can study the market and figure out the right timing on the trade, you can, as someone said, "get rich beyond the dreams of avarice."

Q: In your analysis of the cattle market, how do you determine which months you will spread?

Jeff: Whether I make the bet in the front or in the back depends on a lot of specific variables that I will have to watch materialize.

Q: So these are all tactical and management decisions that you have to make after you have adopted a directional bias?

Jeff: Right, but again the decision as to the direction of the market is the easiest one of all.

Q: It can only go up or down!

Jeff: Right. Most people spend all their time on the easy decision. The much more difficult decision involves timing. It reminds me of a story that I tell about Roy Simmons. Roy, as you know, is a legendary Chicago trader. At one time he was reputedly the largest independent commodity trader in the country. Roy allegedly never made less than $1 million for 40 or 50 years as a trader. Once on the trading floor I was looking over his shoulder—I'm really good at reading over peoples' shoulders. I saw him pull this one card out of his pocket and he's staring at this card. I'm wondering to myself, what's he looking at? And then I read it; big as life, one word on an otherwise blank trading card. All it said was *timing.* He put the card back in his pocket and made a trade. I thought about that for a long time and thought to myself, by God, that was something good to know!

Q: When people look for the Holy Grail in trading, it's things like that that are essential.

Jeff: Well, of course that's true. The so-called Holy Grail still requires a knowledge of oneself and personal discipline.

Q: How do you analyze the cattle market in relation to other livestock markets? For example, the hog market has had an extraordinarily good run recently and the breeding cycle is a lot different than the cattle cycle. How do you use that kind of information in your spread analysis?

Jeff: Well, yeah. Historically there was a period where we were in the middle of the end of a liquidation phase in the cattle cycle, and at the same time, we were in the middle of a high price phase of the hog cycle. And at that time, I scratched my head, thinking, "You know, the only thing that could be bearish on cattle prices would be if hogs would go down a lot." And I said, "Gee! I know now how to hedge against hogs going down a lot! You could sell them!" I bought cattle and sold hogs near even money and I rode it out for 20 cents ($8,000 per contract) from January 15 to April 1. It was a funny year, and I was so supremely confident with the position that I thought there was somebody standing in front of me to take delivery. I was shocked when I learned I got delivery of 200 to 300 loads of April cattle; I was down in Palm Beach vacationing. All the commercials were waiting for me to puke my lunch in the pit the next day, because they knew that I didn't know anything about taking delivery. I proceeded to call all my friends and told them that I was going to take the cattle out to the feedlots; we're going to hang onto them. All the locals were preparing to buy the market 100 lower. When I wasn't there to sell it, the market ended up going limit up of course, but I was gone a short time after that. I was able to let's say, sneak out. It was one of the nicest trades I've ever had.

There's a situation in the hog market today where we've had extremely high corn prices in March and April and that's certainly leading to low hog supplies, you know, eight to ten months out. And the fact that we had very low hog prices in the fall of '94 and early '95 is compounding the situation. Currently, hog prices are high, and the hog-corn ratio is relatively high compared to what it's been in recent history. I suspect that by late summer we're going to be seeing massive increases in marketable hogs. The problem with the scenario is, the pricing structure of the market's very efficient. There's no surprise out there. The back-month hogs are priced at levels that have fully discounted the probable increase of supplies. So it makes it very difficult to do something. It's not like the market's about to make a huge mistake. You know, that's one of the things that I've often tried to do as a speculator. It's profitable not to go with the crowd. It's profitable to figure out what everybody else doesn't know, the subtlety, the fact of life that they're overlooking. Most traders are only looking at the things that happened in the last cycle or the last year or the last part of the cycle; whereas, if it were that easy to profitably analyze the spread relationships, there would be tons of economists working at agricultural schools who would be multimillionaires. The last time I looked, very few of those people were immensely successful as speculators. It takes something of a more pragmatic approach and an ability to see what is invisible to the rest of the pack.

Q: In your normal course of trading, would you say that the majority of your analysis and trades are intermarket, which is to say you look for the intermarket differentials between cattle and hogs or wheat and corn rather than just trade a single market or spread relationship within a single market?

Jeff: Typically I try to evaluate all potential trades in the universe of markets with which I'm comfortable. I'll define a group of trades that I think has potential and then specifically define how opportunity gets expressed, whether it's with a spread or an outright trade. Often, it is to take advantage of a price move in an intermarket trade that will exploit a price movement from two separate although related commodities. I also assign arbitrary noise-related internal "Jeffrey margin requirements" that are substantially greater than the exchange minimums.

Q: You spoke earlier about the fundamental situation that currently exists in the cattle market and the fact that you see the potential of a $20 move materializing. Why spread?

Jeff: Well, in a way we're back to "don't diddle in the middle." At the early stages of the move, perhaps the best way to capture profit is through an outright position. But once you get into the middle phase of something that may take two years to manifest itself, the risk becomes greater. The more correct your analysis, the further you get from that home base of the low $60s. And it's in that area where there are incentives to explore ways of taking advantage of the trade with lower noise, where you can utilize the enhanced leverage of spreading that has a better risk profile than an outright position.

Q: Do you find personally from a psychological perspective that adopting a spread strategy allows you to more comfortably take on risk?

Jeff: I think you're hitting on an interesting point. Big money in the markets is made off the floor. Big money is made by the traders who adopt long-term positions. To trade with a long-term position, you have to be comfortable and be able to withstand the day-to-day fluctuations in price. You don't want to have to look at things every second of the day. For me, I don't want to be glued to the screen. Spreading is not a panacea, but it lets me be a long-term position trader and sit through much more market noise and be comfortable, allowing the market to express the underlying market variables.

Q: Do you think spreaders have a greater longevity than outright traders?

Jeff: I think, once again we're back to the topic of "edge." If you're just going to trade one month of the market and just buy or sell without considering other options, you're embarking on a path without a full set of tools. It's like going hunting with a bow and arrow with a quiver that contains only one arrow. I'd like to have a lot of arrows and have a choice of things that I can utilize to accomplish my final goal, which is to me the largest amount of money that is possible on a given trade. There is one other point here that I would like to underscore

It's one of the key lessons that I had to learn after 16 years in the wilderness. I read it in an essay by a famous cotton speculator who was a chairman of the New York Cotton Exchange, Dickenson G. Watts. Watts wrote always "Sell down to the sleeping level." You probably don't know what that means unless you've had a position that was way too big.

I believe you reach some level of maturity in the futures market when you know how big a position you should take on. Stress manifests itself in waking up in the middle of the night and worrying about it, night sweats if you will. You know, I'm almost 51, and aside from the fact I'm taking some vitamins that might tend to keep my skin a little oily, I still break out in adolescent acne when I'm under a lot of stress, usually caused by a large position. I use that as a signal that I've got too much emotion involved in a trade. It's something every trader has to be aware of.

Q: When you've got to take out the Clearasil, it's time to get rid of the position!

Jeff: Exactly!

Q: What role do you think technical analysis plays in spread trading?

Jeff: Howard, being a fundamentalist, the use of technical analysis in my mind is not to get you direction; it's to get you timing! From this perspective, timing involves identifying climaxes: the extreme of price based on price history. There are various indicators that people use to identify price extremes. The relative strength index or RSI is one of the simplest ones. I use a combination of open interest and the CFTC's (Commodity Futures Trading Commission) report called *Commitments of Traders*. I look at the market statistics for the numbers of advisers that are bullish and bearish.

In addition, I look at moving averages to see what the technical trend following computerized commodity trading funds is doing and look at oscillators that indicate overbought and oversold conditions. Once I've figured out a direction and establish technical indicators that give me timing, then I'm pretty much ready to go. I also like to survey the attitudes of traders, and when they're all bearish, and they're looking for a big increase in supply in the very near future, and there are fundamental reasons that my analysis tells me that things aren't going to be as bad as everybody thinks, that's when I feel I have all my ducks in a row and the confidence that, although everything looks terrible, opportunity is close by. You know, it's raining cats and dogs, and I say to myself, this is a great time to sell umbrellas. Or I might say it is a great time to take my bucket outside and fill it up.

Q: What word of advice would you give to the aspiring spread trader?

Jeff: First of all, and most importantly, more so than any technical or fundamental analysis, you've really got to know yourself and be convinced that you want to climb this mountain to take this journey. If you do, you must devote the time and effort that spreading requires. Also, have enough money set aside that you can learn by making your own mistakes. Join a trading club, be part of an operation where you can meet and talk with other traders. Use the Internet. There are lots of links there. You'll get out of trading what you put into it. It sounds so trite, but it's all too true.

Q: Buy low, sell high still sounds trite, too.

Jeff: To the extent that you're willing to put the time and money into spread trading the potential profits will pay you for all your efforts. The one thing I do advise people to be extraordinarily careful about are all the advertised sure-fire systems and sure-fire methods. You know, you've seen them: You don't have to do any work; just five minutes a day and you'll make millions. These people must be a whole lot smarter than me, because it took me 20 years and a lot of hard study to figure out this game. Nobody else's system can work for you, because your individual makeup is different. Your tolerance for risk, your desire for excitement, your willingness to put time and resources into the study and the acquisition of knowledge. Bottom line, success or failure resides with you!

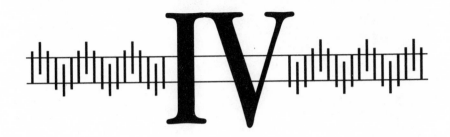

Winning
versus
Losing

CHAPTER 12

How Winning Spread Traders Think

In this chapter, I offer the writings and opinions of some of the individuals that Bob Koppel and I interviewed between 1989 and 1996 when we had the privilege to speak with many of the world's top traders and market experts. I believe these ideas offer a considerable resource to spread traders to improve their performance.

Leo Melamed

Leo Melamed is chairman emeritus of the Chicago Mercantile Exchange and is an active futures trader and chairman and CEO of Sakura Dellsher, Inc., a futures commission merchant. In his first term as chairman of the CME from 1969 to 1971, Melamed was instrumental in pioneering the concept of foreign currency futures and in creating the International Monetary Market—the first futures market for financial instruments. Melamed is the former chairman of the Globex Corporation, which, beginning in 1990, became the electronic system for the Chicago Mercantile Exchange. He has been an adviser to the Commodity Futures Trading Commission and has lectured and written extensively on the subject of financial futures markets. Melamed is the editor of *The Merits of Flexible Exchange Rates: An Anthology* (University Publishing Associates, 1988) and the author of *Leo Melamed on the Markets* (Wiley, 1992) and his new book, *Back to the Futures.*

Here's what Leo Melamed said when asked what it takes to become a successful trader:

"I've been asked that a thousand times. There is no clear answer. I think it's the psychological makeup of the person more than anything else. Clearly, if you're trained to be a trader, it helps. If you're educated, it helps. If you've got money, it helps. If you're tall and got good elbows in the pit, it helps. But all of those things don't help enough! The main element is your own psychological makeup! It has to be a psychology that allows you not to have any ego. A person with ego cannot be a successful trader, because there are times when you are wrong! If your ego prevents you from saying and admitting to yourself, 'I am wrong,' then you'll be defeated, you'll lose, you will go broke! You have to have a personality that is always honest with yourself. You cannot be influenced by what someone else is doing— 'Maybe he knows things I don't know and he's buying so I should be buying.' That's not how you become a good trader."

"Yes, a good trader has to be honest with himself. What do I believe is the central question? Do I believe that this market's going up? Do I believe this market's going down? On the basis of what I see, on the basis of what I know, I have to be honest with myself. If that opinion is wrong, I have to admit it to myself as quickly as possible. It's a psychology of wanting to win. Wanting to be right and being willing to admit defeat to yourself in order that you can be right the next time."

"It requires a risk taker's mentality. I mean, there are people who simply cannot take a risk. They have to put their money into Treasury bills; they want their interest and that's all."

"One of them is the ability to take a loss. You've got to know that no risk taker is going to be right all the time. As a matter of fact, I figured out when I was trading that I could be wrong 60 percent of the time and come out a big winner. The key is money management. You must take your losses quickly and keep them small and let your profits run and make them worthwhile. In that fashion, you could be wrong 60 percent of the time and have a big result because you'll make a lot more money the 40 percent of the time that you are right."

"A lot of people just can't face the fact that they're wrong. So, you need these two elements. First of all, the willingness to take a risk. And the other thing is the ability to admit that you are wrong. There is also a third element. You must isolate your emotions. Don't let the emotion of a loss carry over to your next trade, because then you'll surely ruin the next trade!

"Each trade has to be independent on its own. You cannot let a previous defeat affect the next attempt. If you do, you've got a mission to vindicate your previous loss. That should never be the psychology of a trader. Each trade has to stand on its own merits, on its own two feet, and once it's over, it's over."

Jack Sandner

In January 1993, Jack Sandner began a record ninth year as chairman of the Chicago Mercantile Exchange. A pivotal industry leader, Sandner played a critical role in the development of Globex, the international after-hours, electronic trading system. Sandner, formerly a trial attorney, joined the CME in 1971 and has served continuously on its governing board since 1977. He has served on and chaired scores of member committees. In 1978 he became president and CEO of RB&H, Inc., a futures commission merchant and clearing member firm of the CME. Sandner has long had a national reputation as a futures trader.

"You have to constantly pay attention to exactly what you're doing and what your trading plan is and rigorously focus on it. That's where the discipline is instinctive, but for most traders it is not. I think people who have suffered adversity and have overcome it many times are able to become good traders. I can think of countless times in trading where things were adverse, but, if I didn't have the right attitude, I would have crumbled and walked away and never been able to come back."

"I think you have to do a self-evaluation of whether you have the personality profile to be a trader, or the potential personality profile to be a trader."

"The key to successful trading is the ability to focus, have confidence in yourself, be disciplined and allow yourself to accept adversity (limited risk)."

Jeffrey L. Silverman

Jeffrey L. Silverman is an independent trader and member of the Chicago Mercantile Exchange. He currently serves on and was elected to the position of secretary of the CME's Board of Directors. He has 25 years' experience trading a broad range of financial and physical derivatives.

Silverman holds a bachelor of science degree from the Massachusetts Institute of Technology, concentrating on economics and finance, and studied with Paul Samuelson and Paul Cootner (random walk theorist). He was associated with Commodities Corp. in its formative stages. Silverman describes himself as an active student of the philosophy, psychology, and general theory of markets.

"There are two primary psychological barriers. One is lack of discipline and the other is inflexibility. Inflexibility is an inability to recognize when the market has turned. For example, a person gets in a position where he tells himself that he has developed a disciplined trading style where he's going to sit with that position through thick and thin, waiting for it to grow to fruition. I'm talking as a long-term position trader where I have gravitated. It seems to me that this is where the serious money is made. That very discipline of sticking to a position at some point creates the situation where you can put your head in the sand and ignore the negative evidence in your position. What I'm also saying is you have to have the flexibility, while you're sticking and staying, to be able to turn around and look at it and say, gee, I may be wrong here, and then get out! That flexibility not to go down with sinking ships separates the winners from the losers. It's a discipline to have a plan. Be unemotional about getting in. Be unemotional about the position and be unemotional about getting out.

"You must spend the time—you must study the characteristics of successful traders. You must study your mistakes. You must study the mistakes of the others around you. Increasing levels of sophistication will put you in the direction of understanding who you are. You must really study your own self and understand what you're all about. It's not clear to me whether I didn't do this whole thing backwards, where I studied the economics and science of trading and worked into the philosophical thinking of the whole trading process. It's not clear to me that I should have studied philosophy and psychology at the start and it might have made the whole process easier. I look at what I think the risk is in a position. I look at what I think the return is likely to be. I try to maximize what's in my account in terms of the most bang for the buck, in terms of return for risk and in terms of return for margin-dollar investment. Then, as

I've gotten more successful, I tend to just keep dialing down the amount of risk per margin-dollar so that I can trade with an even longer-term perspective."

Anthony J. Saliba

Anthony J. Saliba is the managing general partner of Saliba Partners. He began his career in the financial industry as an independent market maker at the Chicago Board Options Exchange, Chicago Board of Trade, and Chicago Mercantile Exchange. Saliba is CEO of International Trading Institute (ITI), where he developed a revolutionary voice-activated trading simulator.

"You have to have a plan, a strategy that has a beginning, middle, and an end, and that strategy has to make sense!

"Look both ways before you cross the street! I've heard it a million times, but you know what? I almost got hit by a car the other day. I was walking across Franklin, talking on the telephone with a trader upstairs, and I didn't notice that the light had changed. A car just came down off the ramp, honked his horn and missed me by about two or three feet. It scared the hell out of me! My little four-year-old nephew said, 'Uncle Tony, stop, look, and listen, right?' It's a cliché. How many traders follow the market truths?

"If you're Morgan or Banker's Trust, you still have to know your risk. You've got to watch that you're not at 150 million or 200 million. And if you're a trader at the Merc, and $10,000 or $20,000 is the limit that you can risk during the day, you must stick to your discipline and button it up at that point and be prepared to move on.

"I think the winning strategy for me is to stick to an options trading strategy that I feel comfortable with, because of my personality, and to have quantified risk. Even in a worst-case scenario, if we have Armageddon, we still have it quantified. And within that framework I try to exploit the opportunities that come to me on a trade-by-trade basis. Also, I don't over-trade.

"Now, that alone isn't the recipe for someone to be success-ful. You cannot just go out and copy what I'm doing! Those who are somewhat in the know will understand what I'm talk-ing about. You have to find your own way. However, my advice would be to go out and get yourself a sound pricing model and trade every time you get a signal. I don't think initially that there is much more art involved in it than that. I can say that because, basically, we look for lots of trades and lots of mispric-ing in a number of our accounts. Then in some of our accounts we're looking at the more long-term, and right now you're catching me at the beginning of dabbling in new emerging markets. So we're doing our trading in an old-fashioned way, a Wild-West way. But the same rules apply: Watch your entry, quantify your risk and take it on a trade-by-trade basis."

Mark Douglas

Mark Douglas is president of Trading Behavior Dynamics, Inc., a Chicago-based consulting firm that works with individ-ual traders, CTAs (Commodity Trading Advisors) and brokerage firms. He is the author of *The Disciplined Trader: Developing Winning Attitudes* (New York Institute of Finance, 1989).

"At some point, it will probably occur to you that your trad-ing is simply a feedback mechanism to tell you how much you like yourself at any given moment. After you have learned to trust yourself to always act in your best interests, the only thing that will hold you back is your degree of self-valuation.

"The more positively you feel about yourself, the more abun-dance that will naturally flow your way as a by-product of these positive feelings. So, in essence, to give yourself more money as a trader, you need to identify, change, or discharge anything in your mental environment that doesn't contribute to the high-est degree of self-valuation that is possible. What's possible?

Stay focused on what you need to learn, do the work that is necessary, and your belief in what is possible will naturally expand as a function of your willingness to adapt.

"There are certain characteristics of a mind-set that I believe are essential to creating success in the markets or creating consistency. To me, success as a trader is consistency. There is an often-used saying on the floor of the exchanges that traders just rent their winnings. As you know, there are many traders who have reached the stage of development where they can put together a substantial string of winning trades for days, weeks or even months, only to lose all or most all of their hard-won equity in a few trades and then start the process all over. If a trader hasn't neutralized his susceptibility to give his winnings back to the market, then he is not what I define as a successful trader.

"I know it may sound strange to many readers, but there is an inverse relationship between analysis and trading results. More analysis, or being able to make more distinctions in the market's behavior, will not produce better trading results. Many traders find themselves caught in this exasperating loop, thinking that more or better analysis is going to give them the confidence they need to achieve success. It's what I call a trading paradox that most traders find difficult, if not impossible, to reconcile, until they realize you can't use analysis to overcome your fears of being wrong or losing money. It just doesn't work!"

Charles Faulkner

Charles Faulkner, a certified NLP (neuro-linguistic programming) trainer, is coauthor of the video programs, *NLP: The New Technology of Achievement* and *NLP in Action*. He was interviewed by Jack Schwager in *New Market Wizards* (Harper Business, 1992) about his work with top traders.

"I have this five-point checklist to identify someone who is oriented toward becoming a successful trader. Then Ed Seykota offered me the short version. Look in the mirror and say to yourself, 'I am a trader.' Do you believe it? Here are the other questions to ask: Is trading suited to your lifestyle? Is it something you really enjoy? As Tom Baldwin says, 'Everybody would like to have the money, but who is willing to do the work?' And the work is tremendous! It is a huge commitment that you would only want to do if you loved it. Do you delight in thinking about how the market works, or would you really enjoy playing the game even if you lost because you got to play? You have to have the feeling that you have to be in the game. It's that kind of underlying desire that I think carries people through.

"As I mentioned in my interview with Jack Schwager, you need an edge and you need the mental and emotional flexibility, including not only how you look at the markets but how you think internally. Also, what kinds of beliefs do you have about yourself and your ability? After it's over, how do you look at your accomplishments? And finally, the operating metaphor is the mind-set of the trader, which organizes those beliefs and values into a complete persona that he brings to the markets.

"Ed Seykota among others has mentioned that he makes incredible sums of money for making very, very simple decisions. When one of the 'Turtles' revealed how Richard Dennis really traded, the Donchian channel breakout, these students of Dennis were astonished. They were asking, That's it? That's how this guy makes $200 million? And the answer was, yes.

"This is where I think NLP has made an important contribution not only in trading but across our culture. People are beginning to realize that there is a vast difference between understanding and performance. I think it is finally beginning to sink in! It doesn't matter how many trading books you have read or how much you've studied something. The ability to trade, the ability to perform in a sport or speak a foreign language or drive a car is a matter of practice, experience, and knowledge. Making it more complicated does not make it better.

"You learn to ski by skiing. You learn to trade by trading. The analogy is particularly useful when you recall learning to ski: You started on small hills and perhaps even on special skis. You built up a foundation of ski experience that paved the way for blue and black-diamond runs. The inexperienced trader can learn a lot about trading and risk management by trading anything or by small-stakes gambling. In fact, many of today's great traders got their starts in just this way. Contrary to what the educational process in this country has tried to get us to believe, you don't learn to live your life. You live your life and you learn."

CHAPTER 13

Principles of Successful Spread Trading

Principles of Successful Spread Trading

The following are important principles for successful trading:

- Define your loss.
- Believe in yourself and in unlimited market possibilities.
- Have a well-defined money management program.
- Don't buy tips.
- Don't trade angry or euphoric.
- Trade aggressively at your numbers and points.
- Focus on opportunities.
- Consistently apply your day trading system.
- Be highly motivated.
- Don't overtrade.
- Never average a loss.
- Take small losses, big profits.
- Have no bias to either side of the market.
- Preserve capital.

- Think in probabilities.
- Always trade in a highly positive and resourceful state of mind.
- Act with certainty.
- The market is never wrong.

On the Nature of Becoming a Successful Trader

In order to become a successful spread trader you must be able to do the following:

- Know your outcome.
- Develop a plan of action.
- Reevaluate and retool.

Know Your Outcome

You must have an end point in mind. It is important that you know exactly, in detail, what you want to accomplish in quantifiable and verifiable terms. "I want to become a successful trader and for me this means . . . and I'll know I'm successful when . . ."

Develop a Plan of Action

You must develop a program, a personal strategy to accomplish this end, based on homework, hard work, and discipline.

Reevaluate and Retool

Successful trading, like success itself, is not a single mountain to be climbed or a static "thing" to be possessed. If you want to succeed at trading, it must be viewed as a process, a continuously changing dialogue of the mind, fraught with peril but offering great rewards. So you must be able to adjust to changing conditions. When things work, use them; when they don't, discard them and move on. There are untold riches to be gained in the futures markets, but you need the sensory acuity to be able to discern between winning and losing strategies, and to act accordingly. Have you ever observed a toddler who is in the process of learning to walk? The child employs a host of strategies before he or she is successful. You must view success at trading with the same perspective of flexibility and persistence.

What All Traders Share in Common

All traders, from the novice to the most highly successful, have these things in common: they lose, get frustrated, at times feel lousy, and experience stress and disappointment. But the top traders, at varying points in their careers, undertook to develop personal strategies for overcoming these types of setbacks. They taught themselves specific, however varying, methods for getting around potentially disabling psychological bends in the road, techniques and strategies that you can learn, too.

Wanting to become a winning trader in psychological terms is not very different from choosing to make any significant improvement in your life (e.g., getting in shape). It requires a four-part process which we call the four cs of top trading:

- Commitment
- Conviction
- Constructing new patterns of behavior
- Conditioning

Commitment

All significant change begins with a strong overriding motive to succeed. Picture the intensity of Michael Jordan, Pete Rose, or Magic Johnson. Top-performing traders have a commitment to overcome any hardship or setback to achieve their goals. They also are not afraid to play the game.

There is a wonderful anecdote about a poor overworked guy who goes to church and prays.

"Please, Lord," he incants, "Let me win the lottery."

A week goes by and nothing happens. That Sunday, the man returns to church and once again prays, "Dear Lord, would it really hurt you if I won the lottery?" Still there is no winning number.

Six months pass and the man, determined to win the lottery and having great faith in the power of prayer, returns to church and in his most impassioned, supplicating voice, looking heavenward begins, "Oh, Lord. If only you could let me win this week's lottery."

Suddenly he is interrupted in midprayer by a divine voice that emanates from the church rafters.

"John," begins the voice, "You've gotta buy a ticket!"

It's the same thing with trading. If you want to succeed, you have to buy a ticket. Commitment is your entrance pass.

Conviction

Have you ever observed young children trying to drive their parent's car? They bounce up and down, to and fro in front of the steering wheel. In their mind, they believe their movements will dictate the movement of the car; but the car stands still because it needs a key to turn on the ignition. When it comes to operating in the marketplace, developing a system of beliefs that fosters excellence is the ignition necessary to fire up the engine of great trading. It is critical for you to possess a range of positive beliefs about yourself and success in the market in order to achieve optimum result. As Bruce Johnson put it, "You gotta believe the markets exist just so you can make money."

Constructing New Patterns of Behavior

If you want to lose weight, you have to stop eating french fried potatoes and drinking ice cream sodas. There's no way around it! You must interrupt old patterns of behavior and substitute them with new ones. If you have trouble taking losses in the market or buying when everyone else is selling, or catching breakouts, guess what you have to do to become more successful! Top traders have developed techniques for constructing new patterns of behavior that empower them to act decisively and automatically. So can you!

Conditioning

Finally, once a new pattern of winning behavior has been substituted for a losing one, it is not enough to apply this new approach just once. You must condition yourself—to buy breaks/sell rallies, buy your numbers, trade your system. In short, you must discipline yourself, literally condition your nervous system to act automatically and unemotionally. Discipline does and will produce confidence and ultimate success.

What I have sought to accomplish in *Spread Trading* is to persuasively demonstrate to the reader that, although the specific tactical and strategic skills that are required for spread trading are different from those needed for outright trading, the essential ingredients for success in trading are the same: discipline, patience, motivation, belief in oneself, the ability to identify opportunities and the confidence to exploit those opportunities aggressively when they present themselves. It is these characteristics of belief, thought, and action that are held in common by the world's most successful traders.

Clearly, understanding the fundamental factors that affect spread relationships as well as possessing knowledge of the technical indicators and indices that identify price action, momentum, and volatility are important; however, consistently profitable spread trading involves much more. It is for this reason that I have once again placed such great emphasis not on technique, but rather on the individual trader's attitudes and beliefs about himself or herself, and the market. Therein lies the keys to the treasure chest.

Success in trading!

INDEX

A

Action, automatic, 38
Agatstein, Gene, 19
Anxiety, 23
Attitude, self-defeating, 7–8
Auditory imagery, 13

B

Backwardation, 144, 145
Baldwin, Tom, 185
Barriers, psychological, 15–19
   euphoric trading, 17
   getting "Boston-strangled," 17
   getting locked into a belief,
     16–17
   hesitating your numbers, 18
   inconsistency, 18
   investment in "being right," 18
   kamikaze trading, 17
   lack of well-defined money
     management program, 19
   not catching a breakout, 18
   not defining a loss, 16
   not focusing on opportunities,
     18
   not taking a loss or profit, 16
   wrong state of mind, 19
Berra, Yogi, 17
Buy areas, predetermining, 32

C

Cattle market, 167–69
   in relation to hog market,
     169–70
Churchill, Winston, 25

Coan, F. McCoy, 105–14
   advantages and disadvantages
     of spreading, 110–11
   advice to new traders, 113–14
   buy signals, determining,
     111–12
   consistency of spreading, 113
   early trading experiences,
     105–6
   fundamental information, use
     of, 107–8, 109
   on longevity of traders,
     112–13
   market approach, 106–7, 108
   spread differentials and, 109
   on technical analysis, 114
   trading example (soybean
     meal), 107–9
Commitment, 190
Commitments of Traders, 173
Computer-generated numbers, 37
Conditioning, 191–92
Confidence, 12
Consistency, 25, 184
Conviction, 190–91
Crude oil, 144
Cyclical
   information, 30
   spread relationships, 63–64.
     See also Spread tables,
     seasonal/cyclical/historical

D

Day Trader's Advantage, The, 26
Dennis, Richard, 185
Differential, 134–35
Discipline, 126, 181

Disciplined Trader, The: Developing Winning Attitudes, 183
Douglas, Mark, 183–84

E

Edge
    factors in determining, 8–10, 166
    maintaining an, 31
    strategy and, 24
Elliott waves, 36
Emotions, isolation of, 179
Euphoric trading, 17
Eurodollar(s)
    Fed policy and, 123
    five-year bundle, 155–56, 158
    opportunity, 124
    packs, 159
    patterns, 122–23
    trading example, 117–19

F

Faulkner, Charles, 184–86
Fibonacci ratios, 36
Five-year bundle, 155, 158
Focus, 12, 23, 139, 180
Fundamental information, 30
Fundamentals, 106

G

Gann lines, 36
Globex, 179
Goal setting, 11, 23
Goldman Sachs index, 144
Grains, 146–47

H

Heating oil, 144–45
Hedging, 29
High-percentage trades, 31
Highs and lows, 36, 59

Historical spread relationships, 63–64. *See also* Spread tables, seasonal/cyclical/historical
Hog market, 147–48
    in relation to cattle market, 169–70

I

Inconsistency, 18
Inflexibility, 181
Intercommodity spread, 4
Interest rates, 162
Intermarket spread, 4
International Trading Institute, 182
Intracommodity spread, 4
Investment Psychology Explained, 3

K–L

Kamikaze trading, 17
Kinesthetic imagery, 14
Losses, 16, 134–35, 179

M

McGuire, John, 115
Margin requirements, 165
Market analysis, 29–38
    categories of market awareness, 33–36
    dull/nonperforming markets, avoiding, 32
    innergame approach, 33–36
    preparation, 37–38
    price difference between markets, 29–30
    technical trading tools and, 30
    trading map, creating, 36–37
Market entry and exit, 30
Market retracements, 36
Melamed, Leo, 177–79
Miller, Girard, 127–39
    advice to new traders, 138
    background, 127–28
    early trading experiences, 128–30

factors for success, 138–39
focus and, 139
on longevity of traders,
137–38
market approach, 130–31
on technical analysis, 131
trading example (forward
spread), 132–33
Money management, 19, 26, 30,
165–66
Moore, Steve, 141–52
advice to new traders, 152
attraction to spread trading,
147
early trading experiences, 142
market approach, 146
on psychological aspects of
trading, 149
trading example (hogs),
148–49
Moore Research Center, Inc, 30,
63, 143
Motivation, 11, 22
Mueller, Gene, 128

N–O

Newhouse, John, 115–26
advantages of spread trading,
120
advice to new traders, 125
discipline and, 126
early trading experiences,
115–17
on longevity of traders, 125
market approach, 117
spread relationships, 123–24
success and, 126
technical vs. fundamental
analysis, 120–21
trading example (Eurodollars),
117–19
trends and, 121–22
New Market Wizards, 184
*New Technology of Achievement
and NLP in Action, The,* 184

NLP (neuro-linguistic
programming), 184
Noise, 32
Nordstrom Corporation, 22
Opportunities, 18, 38
anticipation of, 31
strategy and, 25

P

Patience, 31
Pattern recognition, 37, 61
Patterns of behavior, 191
Personality, developing strategy
consistent with, 23
Ponoroff, Charlie, 127
Pork bellies, 147–48
Positive attitude, 183
Positive imagery, 12–13
Pring, Martin, 3
Production cost, and price
structure, 142–43
Profit orientation, 25
Psychology, of trader, 134, 178

R

Risk management, 24
Risk-taker mentality, 179
Robbins, Anthony, 25

S

Sakura Dellsher, Inc., 177
Saliba, Anthony J., 182–83
Sandner, Jack, 179–80
Schwager, Jack, 184
Seasonal
information, 30
patterns, 146
spread relationships, 63–64.
See also Spread tables,
seasonal/cyclical/historical
Segal, George, 16
Self-defeating attitudes, 7–8
Self-honesty, 178
Self-valuation, 183
Sell areas, predetermining, 32
Seykota, Ed, 185

Siegel, Joe, 143
Silverman, Jeffrey L., 163–74, 180–82
  advice to new traders, 173–74
  early trading experiences, 163–64
  market approach, 167–69
  on money management, 165–66
  on psychological aspects of trading, 172
  on risk management, 164
  on technical analysis, 173
Simmons, Roy, 169
Soybean meal, trading example, 107–9
Soybeans, 146–47
Sperandeo, Vic, 10
Spread relationships, 33–34
Spread tables, seasonal/cyclical/historical, 64–102
Spread trader(s) *See also* Spread trading
  becoming a successful, 188–89
  common experiences of, 189–92
  emotions and, 179
  longevity of, 112–13, 125, 137–38
  personality of, 180
  psychological makeup of, 178
  risk and, 179
  self-honesty and, 178
Spread trading
  advantages and disadvantages of, 110–11, 120, 156
  common types of, 4–5
  defined, 29
  edge, determining, 8–10
  interest rates and, 162
  keys to successful, 6–8
  market analysis and. *See* Market analysis
  preparation for, 37–38
  principles of successful, 187–88

psychological
  barriers to successful, 181
  skills required for successful, 11–14, 189–92
  strategy, 5–6, 21–25
  technical considerations, 26, 30
State of mind, 12, 19
  resourcefulness and, 24
Strategy
  elements of a successful, 21–25, 182–83
  reasons for not adopting a, 5–6
Support and resistance areas, 36
Syntax, of successful trading, 7

T

Technical system or approach, 26, 109, 120–21, 125, 131, 173
Teller, Margery, 153–62
  on advantages/disadvantages of spread trading, 156–57
  advice to new spread traders, 161
  on discipline, confidence, and focus, 160
  early trading experiences, 153–54
  market approach, 154
  on psychological aspects of trading, 157
  trading example (five-year bundle), 155–56
Tips, 17
Trader Vic: Methods of a Wall Street Master, 10
Traders. *See* Spread trader(s)
Trading Behavior Dynamics, 183
Trend, 30, 36–37, 60–61

V–W

Visual imagery, 13
Watts, Dickenson G., 172
Winning state of mind, 7

Howard Abell is chief operating officer of the Innergame Division of Rand Financial Services, Inc., concentrating on brokerage and execution services for institutional and professional traders. Rand Financial Services, Inc., is a Chicago-based futures clearing merchant (FCM) clearing all major world exchanges. Abell is the coauthor, with Bob Koppel, of *The Innergame of Trading* (Irwin, 1993) and *The Outer Game of Trading* (Irwin, 1994). He is the author of *The Day Trader's Advantage* (Dearborn, 1996). Abell currently manages Tao Partners, a Commodity Trading Advisor.

For additional information about Rand Financial Services or Tao Partners, please contact:

Innergame Division/Rand Financial Services, Inc.
Chicago Mercantile Exchange
30 South Wacker Drive
Suite 2200
Chicago, IL 60606
312-559-8898
800-726-3088
fax: 312-559-8848
e-mail: hma@innergame.com
Visit our Website at www.innergame.com.